The Rhetoric of Black Mayors

In Their Own Words

Deborah F. Atwater

University Press of America,® Inc.
Lanham • Boulder • New York • Toronto • Plymouth, UK

Copyright © 2010 by
University Press of America,® Inc.
4501 Forbes Boulevard
Suite 200
Lanham, Maryland 20706
UPA Acquisitions Department (301) 459-3366

Estover Road
Plymouth PL6 7PY
United Kingdom

Library of Congress Control Number: 2010925511
ISBN: 978-0-7618-5076-2 (paperback : alk. paper)
eISBN: 978-0-7618-5077-9

$\otimes^{TM}$ The paper used in this publication meets the minimum
requirements of American National Standard for Information
Sciences—Permanence of Paper for Printed Library Materials,
ANSI Z39.48-1992

This book is dedicated to my mother and father, Samuel and Tessie Atwater, who gave me the love, support, and guidance that I needed to be successful in life.

Contents

Acknowledgments

A special thanks goes to the following people for helping me complete this project.

Dr. Monika K. Alston who helped with some of the earlier research on the
  project
Mr. Arthur Boswell and Mrs. Carolyn Boswell
Mr. Eugene Cannon and Dr. Lillian Cannon
Mr. Vernon Clark
Drs. Robert and Melbourne Cummings
Dr. Dennis S. Gouran who read an earlier draft of this manuscript
Mr. Danny Laws and Mrs. Myra Laws

The Ida B. Wells Women's Writing Circle:
Dr. Christine Clark-Evans and Dr. Beverly Vandiver

Introduction

The political philosophy of Black Nationalism means that the black man should control the politics and the politicians in his community; no more.

Malcolm X
(Janet Cheatham Bell, *Famous Black Quotes*, 56)

Theodore White states, "The American cities are becoming a despair of our civilization. More money has been spent to save our great cities, and more paper covered with reports on those cities, than any other concern in American life. Yet they are desperate, more unsafe and more frighteningly trapped than at any time in our history. These are the centers of American industry and trade, of its arts and culture. What can be done to make them livable for white and black, for the poor and the rich, for the working man and the middle-class?" (*America In Search of Itself: The Making of the President-1956-1980*, 428.)

With the recent Democratic nomination of Illinois Senator Barack Obama as the first African American Presidential nominee of a major political party, and his election to that office, it is fitting to explore the impact and the degree of importance that coalitions have on the political process formed by Black officials in general, and for the purposes of this book, Black Mayors in particular.

The election of hundreds of African-American mayors during the decade following November 1967 was a complex phenomenon that defies simple explanation.[1] The Civil Rights Leader Bayard Rustin predicted the change, positing in a 1965 article that political power would flow from the American Civil Rights Movement. Without the civil rights movement and the political mobilization that it generated, Stokes, Hatcher and others could not have achieved success at the ballot box.

The first Black mayors came into office during intense interracial conflict (particularly following the death of Martin Luther King, Jr.). And while their presence may have somewhat diffused a potentially volatile situation in American cities, "the expectation that black mayors would somehow quickly eradicate the symptoms or the causes of rioting in the burning cities proved unrealistic."[2] Biles describes the entry of Black mayors into office as a difficult one, either because of the resistance of White bureaucratic frameworks already in place or because of the lack of support and help due to the resignation of administrative personnel unwilling to work under a Black mayor. Biles further problematizes the role of the Black mayor through a discussion of severe economic conditions including rising crime and police brutality, and timing. (Many Black mayors were elected to the office at the lowest most perilous point in the city's history.)

Recent Black mayors such as New York City's David Dinkins and Baltimore's Kurt Schmoke were not deterred by these challenges. Rather, they went forward in their bid for the office of mayor of their respective cities and became the avant-garde. Despite the challenges that came with the office, these Black mayors, through their power to appoint city officials, brought into their communities much needed minority set-asides, labor contracts and affirmative action programs.

Group succession fails to explain fully the fortunes of African American mayors. Because of the persistent influence of racism in American urban society, the experience of African American politicians stands apart from those of their ethnic predecessors, particularly with regard to governance itself. Established political institutions proved substantially less flexible for African Americans than for others. This is not to deny the effects of xenophobia, anti-Semitism or other forms of prejudice or group conflict. However, such discrimination was not comparable to social prejudice.[3]

While the increasing rise in elections of African American mayors may have represented a powerful symbolic change, its influence on poverty and inequality appear to have been only modest. Similarly, particular legislative and institutional reforms could be termed minor achievements – or the first rumble in a seismic shift in public policy and political power.[4] In agreement with Jeffrey Adler, I believe that the history of African American mayors cannot be understood apart from the history of the late 20th Century city. Forces such as deindustrialization, White flight, and residential segregation set the stage for the victories of Black mayors and exaggerated the obstacles these executives confronted. Whether the trend begun by Stokes and Hatcher in 1967 continues in this century will depend on the tenor of race relations in the American city.[5] Adler, Biles (1992) substantiates this point by stating the relationship between African-American voting rights to the number of Black candidates for public office. While some Blacks had voting rights in antebellum America, there were no Black candidates for public office prior to the Civil War. Following the Civil War and Reconstruction, Blacks gained a degree of voting power and Black men were elected to city councils in a number of major Southern cities. However, with the passage of Jim Crow laws in the 1880s, public offices were returned to their previously "White-only" status.

Blacks in both the North and the South began supporting the larger political machines in order to gain influence in the political arena and many Black leaders became spokesmen for political machines. Biles (1992) posits that these relationships benefited Black elites and Black politicians more than they benefited the larger community. Following WW II, the population of Blacks grew in major cities and the Black community was able to break away from White political machines and elect a few Black officials to significant political offices. Rev. Adam Clayton Powell of New York is one example of the shift from a subordinate role in the political arena to an increasingly aggressive style of Black leadership in American politics. The 1960's witnesses a significant turning point in the struggle in that the new Voting Rights laws gave Blacks protection and led to the election of a number of Black mayors.

NOTES

1. David R. Colburn and Jeffrey S. Adler, eds., *African-American Mayors: Race, Politics, and the American City* (Urbana and Chicago: University of Illinois Press, 2001), 19-20.
2. Roger Biles, "Black Mayors: An Historical Assessment." *Journal of Negro History.* 77, no. 3 (Summer 1992): 115.
3. Colburn and Adler, *African-American Mayors*, 2-3.
4. Colburn and Adler, *African-American Mayors*, 11.
5. Colburn and Adler, *African-American Mayors*, 19.

Chapter One

Wilson Goode:
Mayor as Technocrat and Pioneer,
Philadelphia, PA

There are over 600 Black mayors in the United States (Black Mayors Conference, 2008). And there have been numerous books and articles about Black mayors. But the rhetorical dimensions have not been examined in depth. Most of the journal articles and books have focused on Mayors Harold Washington, Chicago, Illinois; Carl Stokes, Cleveland, Ohio; Richard Hatcher, Gary, Indiana; and Mayor Tom Bradley, Los Angeles, California. More recently, there has been focus on Mayors Andrew Young and Maynard Jackson, Atlanta, Georgia; Ernest Morial, New Orleans, Louisiana; David Dinkins, New York, New York; and Wilson Goode, Philadelphia, Pennsylvania.

There are those who would argue that politics is now the cutting edge of the American Civil Rights Movement with the greatest success being the election of Black mayors. These Black mayors, especially those of medium to large sized cities have been and continue to be challenged to address and resolve a myriad of urban problems. With these challenges comes a huge responsibility, and in some cases, a burden. As Nelson (1977, 2000) states, "Black mayors, far more so than white, are expected to be activist entrepreneurs, innovative problem solvers who can bring consummate expertise, skill, common sense, and power to bear on pressing social and economic problems."[1] For many, the election of Black mayors has come to symbolize the continuing efficacy of the American Civil Rights Movement—a high responsibility indeed. Unfortunately, it appears that Black mayors are elected to govern and lead dying cities fraught with cumulative ills. Many Black mayors have been placed in charge of sinking ships with little to no resources with which to save their cities.

Historically, one of the major focuses of the American Civil Rights Movement in the 1960s was the exclusion of Blacks from the American political arena. Over twenty years ago, Morrison (1987) stated:

> For our purposes, it is most useful to think of the Montgomery boycott as the catalyst, and Martin Luther King, Jr. as the symbol of evolving mobilization. Voter registration was one of the prime examples of the general confidence and perception of improved social and political prospects on the part of Blacks.[2]

He acknowledged that "Much of the effort of Black Americans to achieve power has been expended in a struggle against the vagaries of white racism--a product and vestige of the enslavement era." Unfortunately, racism continues to exist in various forms; overt, covert and visceral.

Andrew Young argues that the Civil Rights Movement has gone into politics and business and its people (who were formerly leading demonstrations) are now ensconced in city halls. For many, mayors have become the focal point for those who hope to resolve urban problems in cities which now must deal with a generation that has been cut-off from mainstream America. A difficult position indeed! But we cannot afford to neglect or throw away our cities and the people in them.

Black mayors not only have to bring order back to the cities, they have to do it while operating with budgets that have been receiving declining funding from the Federal Government. The aftermath of Hurricane Katrina in New Orleans 2005 reflects the result of inadequate funding—even in the midst of a National disaster. There are those who would argue that perhaps the delayed and insufficient response was caused by a Republican President and Congress. The alarming thing is that allocation of government funds continues to be scarce or practically non-existent for our urban cities even with the 2009 stimulus legislation.

Since the 1967 election of Carl Stokes in Cleveland as the first Black mayor of a major American city, Black mayors have continued to suffer the stigma of the citizens' lack of faith in their political acumen (both Black and White). According to Stokes, "The voices of our critics will be more rancorous. Our failures will be magnified ... Then we will witness the worst of all crises, for our cities will be undone."[3] Adding in 1970, "All first-term mayors believe their election will bring miracles. I am no longer suffering from that illusion."[4] Wilson Goode echoed this opinion twenty-three years later in my interview with him in 1993.

The issue of press coverage and image has been discussed by numerous researchers who believe that Black mayors often serve as national symbols, and the increasing frequency with which they are being elected to political office is widely recognized by the media as an index of their increasing political integration into the mainstream. Yet Riffe, et al. (1990) observed that White press coverage of Black mayors continues to be consistently insensitive, incomplete and inappropriate.

Black mayors may experience symbolic benefits because they represent Black needs and interests in the political process, encourage other Blacks to run for political office and help to modify racial models. In an age of growing urban unrest, Black youth are often more supportive of Black mayors. In addition, Black mayors serve as role models for the entire Black community as their positions continue to reverse traditional images of White superiority.

In order to be successful, many Blacks have had to form coalitions comprised of Black civic reformists; Black nationalists; labor unions; Black entrepreneurs; progressive Latino activists; Black clergy and White liberals. In short, Black candidates must have interracial appeal and thus are learning how to better appeal to White voters who are concerned with the same issues as are Blacks and other minorities. A challenging rhetorical problem for all mayoral candidates and mayors is their ability to keep those groups he/she already has while reaching out to include new and sometimes vastly different groups.

Certainly, there continues to be a wealth of information on Black mayors yet to be explored and discussed if we are to determine their full impact on society. Black officials often bring about real changes that improve the lives of their constituents in vital areas such as jobs, housing; food; health care; day care; education and job training. Additionally, Black officials can often sensitize their White associates. Not only with overt proposals, *but simply by their presence.* And they provide a crucial link between government and Black citizenry in ways that Whites simply cannot. In general, the common belief is that Black mayors are more successful in bringing about changes in *capital-intensive services* which affect the conditions of streets, parking, water and sewage than they are in improving *human resource services* like employment, housing, policies and protection. However, it is likely that the mayors referenced in this book would disagree with this perception.

In reviewing the efforts of Black incumbent mayors in several large U.S. cities, their elections signaled that the era of Black empowerment has not been short lived. Or perhaps it is. With the election of John Street as the second African American mayor of Philadelphia, it is fitting to re-examine his predecessor, African American Mayor Wilson W. Goode. Street's election is significant because it demonstrates what many political scientists and others who follow politics took for granted that the election of a second African American mayor in Philadelphia would not be such a difficult task. Street's election took longer than anyone had anticipated. An examination of Goode and his administration may shed some light as to why the election of a second African American mayor took so incredibly long.

It is within this context that the rhetorical image of W. Wilson Goode, the first African American Mayor of Philadelphia will be discussed. The rhetorical situation of the campaign can be determined by referring to newspaper accounts and data collected in interviews. Rhetorical situation is defined as, "a complex of persons, events, objects, and relations presenting an actual or potential exigence which can be completely or partially removed if discourse, introduced into the situation, can so constrain human decision or action as so to bring about the significant modification of exigence."[5] Generally speaking, communication may be defined as the sending and receiving of messages to organize the environment. Black rhetoric can be defined as a phenomenon of messages both verbal and nonverbal generated by Blacks for Blacks for the attainment of the "good life."[6] It is also the management of symbols to coordinate social action.[7] What better way to coordinate social action than to get people to vote? *Therefore, how an individual manages those symbols becomes important.* Sheridan (1996) raises several important questions: Are the new Black leaders the keepers of King's dream—or betrayers? Do they benefit the Black community at large? Or, is some other community, individual or perhaps the leader himself benefitting? Is the increasing number of Blacks in new and powerful spaces a good thing?

THE ISSUES

To determine how Wilson Goode approached and addressed general and situationally unique issues, I turned to newspaper accounts of the campaign. For the purposes of this inquiry, *general issues* are defined as those usual issues relating to housing; jobs; finances; health services; recreational facilities; neighborhood and downtown redevelopment; public safety improvements in the police department and public transportation. *Situationally unique issues* are those issues unique to Wilson Goode based on his personal history and the political history of Philadelphia. Specifically, what appeals did Mayor Goode use in his campaign rhetoric to build coalitions? Could these serve as a barometer for future attempts at coalition building for other African American mayors?

Referencing local newspapers (Black and White) and information from interviews from appropriate individuals connected with the campaign and information from former Mayor Goode, I was able to assess the rhetorical situation.

PHILADELPHIA—THE CITY OF
BROTHERLY LOVE (AND SISTERLY AFFECTION)

With the election of Wilson Goode in 1983, the voters in the city of Philadelphia realized a goal that had taken some fifteen to twenty years to reach.

W. Wilson Goode came to political power when Congressmen Bill Green appointed Goode as his managing director, fulfilling a campaign promise to hire a Black for the position. When Mayor Green declined to run for re-election, Goode took his place. Running as a highly educated, hardworking, professional manager, he won approximately 23% of the White vote and 97-98% of the Black vote.

Mr. Goode "having once walked behind a mule-drawn plow in North Carolina fields, planted by his sharecropper father, inspired us with his life story."[8] Wilson Goode was preferable to African American Charles Bowser who was too much of an independent, grass-roots candidate. As African American Lucien Blackwell, a well known "rabble-rouser" noted—while Goode was perceived as the candidate who could appeal to a broader audience because he was seen as a non-threatening, technocratic kind of individual steeped in running city government, able to reach out to the White community. In other words, he was a viable, believable mayoral candidate who people believed would be able to unify the city. But we must be clear about the city that Goode inherited. In Goode's own words:

> The Philadelphia I inherited as the city's first African-American Mayor was on the verge of collapse, suffering a slow hemorrhaging death from high inflation, a declining population, and an anemic revenue base created by the exodus of thousands of jobs.[9]

However, in 1987 when he ran against Frank Rizzo, he was suddenly less of a technocrat and more of a politician. He won by a mere 17,000 votes (White support at 70%, 97% Blacks voting for Goode. His support in the White community had decreased as Whites defected to the Republican Party. As Bauman (1992) discusses Goode's first mayoralty, his campaign presented him as a cost-cutting manager rather than as a politician. Bauman argues that Goode's style of management was more effective in a business venue than in a political arena. His management style was one of consulting a variety of people on policy issues (local groups, friends, experts, etc.), retreating to his office to consider the options and then decide on the issue. Bauman also argues that this particular style proved harmful when Goode dealt with the MOVE issue.

> MOVE: MOVE is short for "The Movement" a radical, activist counterculture organization that arose in Philadelphia; some recall its existence as far back as 1968. John Africa, whose birth name was Vincent Leophart, was the founder and philosophical leader of the organization. He was a Black handy man who did carpentry work for a community housing cooperative in the Powelton Village section of West Philadelphia. In return for his services, he was given a small house in the area. MOVE was mostly known as a loose knit, mostly Black

group whose members adopted the surname Africa, advocated a "back-to-nature lifestyle and preached against technology." Following a deadly standoff with police in 1978, nine MOVE members were sentenced to prison for third degree murder. The group came to international attention in 1985 after an attempt by the Philadelphia Police Department to enforce arrest warrants escalated dramatically. The police dropped a bomb from a helicopter onto the roof of the MOVE residence. The resulting fire was allowed to burn. This resulted in the deaths of six adults and five children.[10]

Following the MOVE crisis Goode's political capital went downhill. As a consequence, many in the city felt it would be a long time before another Black candidate would again be elected to the office. It wasn't until 1998 that the second African American, John Street was elected mayor. What crucial event led to Goode's decrease in popularity?

GOODE AND THE MOVE CRISIS

(I was not permitted to ask Mayor Goode about the Move Crisis during our interview. However, his book, *In Good Faith*, 1992 covers the Move Crisis in detail.)

For many of the citizens of Philadelphia, and all of America, May 14, 1985 will be a day that will forever remain etched in their minds. On that day, Philadelphia became the second city in the United States (the other one was Oklahoma City, 1921) in which the government dropped a bomb on its citizens for civil unrest. Russell Cooke's editorial in the January 5, 1992 *Philadelphia Inquirer* states it best in "Exit Mayor Goode, He Began with Great Hope, but His Legacy is One of Failed Leadership and Missed Chances."

It is assumed that no future mayor will have Goode's situationally unique albatross, MOVE. Though he never set foot on Osage Avenue on that spring day in 1985 when a predominately Black West Philadelphia neighborhood burned to the ground and 11 people died, it was he who approved the Police Department's plan of assault. The Black community believed that the appointment of Gregore Sambor as Police Commissioner was a strategic error on the part of Goode because of Sambor's long and negative history with MOVE, but more importantly, because of Sambor's lack of street-level experience. Goode's earlier administration had ignored MOVE's unorthodox behavior of living a return-to-nature existence in the city.

Former Philadelphia Mayor (now Pennsylvania Governor Ed Rendell) said at the time, "MOVE stands as a monument to the mismanagement and incompetence of Wilson Goode."[11] MOVE sent the Goode administration into a tailspin. Goode lost control of the City Council, and those in charge of state funds were given the ammunition needed to continue to bash Philadelphia and dismiss Goode's assessment about the very real financial difficulties facing the city.

Cooke adds, "While he set out to be a hands-on mayor; part civic cheerleader, part nuts-and-bolts manager working 16 hour days, they proved to be no substitute for the behind-the-scenes follow-through that often was lacking on initiatives both big and small. He was left with a credibility gap because he could not deliver on so many of his promises."[12] Cooke specifically refers to one of Goode's campaign promises to have an office in which volunteers would be available to answer citizen's questions; an office which never materialized.

In spite of these devastating circumstances, there were some accomplishments. Under his administration, Goode brought Black and minority leadership to the top levels of municipal government, putting together a cabinet consisting of three women, three Blacks, three Whites, and one Hispanic. Philadelphia's skyline was transformed; the sports teams stayed and the cross-town Vine Street Expressway and I-95 Ramp were completed. He is also credited with the successful ending of the garbage strike in 1986, without breaking the union. But how was Goode's administration playing in the press?

BLACK MAYORS AND THE WHITE PRESS

"I don't know if it's our business to be kind or unkind to anybody. We want to convey a sense of what the reality is out there." (Cooke, 1993)

When the newspaper supports a candidate, a 14 member editorial board decides who that candidate will be. The Editorial Board meets and each member openly votes for the candidate of their choice. The publisher of the newspaper may or may not attend this meeting. In terms of affecting the vote, Cook says, "We think that we can swing 10-20 thousand votes for our endorsement, but in some cases our support could be viewed as the kiss of death."[13]

I was able to get a sense of how the White press covered Wilson Goode by reading articles and interviewing Russell Cooke of the *Philadelphia Inquirer*. By and large, there are those who would argue that the media was fair to Wilson Goode. (Although it should be noted that national coverage was far less kind to him than was the *Philadelphia Inquirer*. [Time, May 16, 1983]). The *Philadelphia Inquirer* labeled Goode's campaign as "dull, boring and humorless." And later that year, *Time* (November 7, 1983) reported that Goode's platform oratory was "breathtakingly dull." Of course it could be argued that the coverage of Wilson Goode drastically changed both *before and after* MOVE. However, most journalists would agree that Wilson won re-election—not on his own merit, but because a vote *for* him was in reality a vote *against* Frank Rizzo. For others, in both the White and Black communities, Goode was perceived as the lesser of two evils.

VOTER EXPECTATIONS AND THE PRESS

During the campaign, Frank Rizzo argued that the papers did not lay a glove on Goode. However, Cooke insists that the *Philadelphia Inquirer's* coverage of Wilson included Goode's record, and that the paper covered all of Goode's remarks so that "the people could draw their own conclusions. We didn't give him a free ride."[14]

During our interview, Cooke acknowledged that Goode felt that he was held to a higher standard, stating "I don't know what perfection is, but Wilson was certainly held to high standards. If you did not ask the right questions, you would not get any extra information and the extra information would give you a total picture of what the truth might be. I'm sure that Wilson thinks he always told the truth."[15] To be sure, Goode confirms, "The measure is not against other mayors, in the job, but perfection. How do you compare to perfection?"[16] But is perfection attainable in any job or profession?

Perhaps, Goode was a victim of the times as well as his own troubles in terms of how he was viewed and scrutinized. It was a time when all politicians found that they too were having the light shown on them as well.

BLACK MAYORS AND THE BLACK PRESS

With the increasing numbers of Black politicians, it is crucial that there be fair and accurate reporting. Customarily, Black newspapers have "served to establish an African identity in the communities that countered the stereotypes perpetuated by the communities as a whole, which were often fostered by the White-owned press.[17] So obvious is the difference in coverage that, "In 1989, political scientist, Robert Entman found that Chicago television news associated black politicians with special-interest politics, portraying them as threatening militants. In contrast, White politicians—even when coming from clear ethnic bases—were presented as if they represented the entire community."[18]

The city of Philadelphia is no different than any other large urban city when it comes to the coverage of Black politicians. Astute Black politicians know this as evidenced by how little Lucien Blackwell used the White press and media in the 1991 Philadelphia mayoral campaign. In fact, Lucien Blackwell, one of the

Black candidates, talked very little to the press. As Phyllis Kaniss notes, "Black candidates had other ways of getting their message out: through the Black radio stations, the *Tribune* (Black newspaper), the clergy, and people on the street."[19]

To ascertain Black press coverage of Wilson Goode, I interviewed Linn Washington, who was the editor of the *Philadelphia Tribune* (Goode also worked at the *Philadelphia Daily News* for ten years [1979-1989]). For Mr. Washington, there were parallel issues in the 1983 campaign. The general issues were housing, employment, and economic development; the situationally unique issue was the empowerment of the Black community. With a concerted effort to get Blacks in powerful positions, what better way to show that empowerment than to elect a Black mayor? Washington agreed with Russell Cook's assessment that based on the numerous battles that Charles Bowser had waged in the preceding years, the time was right for Wilson Goode. States Washington, "The 1983 campaign was a culmination of things and through a strange confluence of events, Wilson Goode was thrust into it, he benefited from a political movement that he really did not have anything to do with."[20] In 1987 there were two other potential Black candidates in addition to Goode, namely City Council President Joe Coleman and John White, Jr., and incredibly, both deferred to Goode. "People were voting against Rizzo not for Goode, even though some thought that Goode appeared to have contempt for grass-roots people."[21]

Washington noted that Wilson did not have a Black agenda but was quick to add that the "Black leadership simply did not come forward to present him with one. All deserve to share the blame; the Blackwells, the Streets, the Richardsons and the Williamsons." Washington feels that Goode could have used his office as a "bully pulpit."[22] This is the dilemma facing Black mayors in most cities. In essence; how do you set and implement an agenda which clearly benefits African Americans in particular and all citizens in general? In other words, how do you keep your Black-based support strong and solid while attempting to appeal to the broader populace?

Goode, acknowledging one dilemma of Black mayors states:

> All cities that are run by African American mayors are in financial crisis that developed over a period of decades. Blacks expect you to fire all whites, bring in all black people, give all contracts to blacks, not all blacks, but some do expect you to do that. The whites expect that you're somehow superman and that all problems that other mayors for 20 years before you could not solve are going to get solved.[23]

One of Goode's failures, the Raymond Rosen Housing Projects, was slated for demolition. While the skyline in Center City was being developed, the minority communities were not being developed. And for many this communicated a negative message regarding Goode's respect and value of grass roots people. Thus, many in the Black community began to question Goode's leadership ability, concluding that he was not a leader, but rather someone who needed to be told what to do. During our interview, Washington said that Goode was enamored with degrees and because of this he had made some questionable appointments because degrees do not necessarily override the need for experience necessary to handle certain jobs. Case-in-point: The appointment of Gregore Sambor to the role of Police Commission. Clearly, Goode missed the opportunity to appoint a Black man or woman as Police Commissioner as well as the opportunity to bring in someone from the outside. In 1983, Wilson benefited from external factors and the Black Press gave him good treatment. But in 1987 the media was more critical. Washington said that "We give Black politicians a little more latitude, a little more sensitivity because we understand the historical context and a lot of this comes out, but there are no free rides. There is an allegiance to grass-roots voters as opposed to the leadership. Just because you're Black don't mean that you're all right. And we have to be sophisticated enough to advance to that point."[24]

BUILDING COALITIONS

In most urban settings, in order to win elections Black coalitions must be built and nurtured. Wilson Goode was keenly aware of this as evidenced by the following statement:

> My coalition was made up of Blacks, white liberals, predominately Jewish liberals, Asians, Hispanics, Russian Jews, and Lithuanians and "other" minorities, but to win, you need a strong Black base and a strong Black agenda. My Black agenda was that I was going to level the playing field. I didn't say Black agenda; I said level the playing field.
>
> I'm going to appoint people throughout all levels of government. This was revolutionary- contracts to minorities, commissioner appointments and appointments to the cabinet. My base grew out of the Black church, because I was not a stranger. I was allowed to speak from the pulpits of Black churches. The Black women organized the Women for Goode group and the Christians for Goode raised a substantial amount of campaign funds.[25]

During the campaign Goode was welcomed to attend those churches because he had frequently visited the churches when he was *not* running for any office which won him favor with this crucial audience. Mr. Goode spoke at Black churches while he was Pennsylvania's Public Utility Commissioner and when he was the city's Managing Director.

In regard to Goode's coalition, Russell Cooke states that, *"In front of cameras, he had a real racial cross section."* However, future coalitions will probably consist of liberals, conservative businessmen from downtown, board members of banks, etc. to save the tax base. But Cook astutely acknowledges that, "*it will always be difficult to get the lower North East, Upper Kensington and Allegheny residents to vote for a Black mayor.*"[26]

Linn Washington observes that "In terms of numbers, we need to have coalitions. We have to appeal to issues but white people never surrender their self-interests. We always do that and that's what Wilson was into. We are satisfied with changes in personnel and personalities as opposed to programmatic changes."[27]

As their comments indicate, all three understand the importance of building effective coalitions.

It is necessary to note that Goode's administration did indeed change the face of government; He positioned many Blacks, (mainly females in the 40 plus age range) and other minorities in key positions. However, most organizations and institutions were headed by middle managers.

So what is Goode's legacy? According to Washington, "He did more, but also 'messed' things up for a successor."[28] As a result, there was sixteen years between Goode's administration and the election of Mayor John Street. It would appear that Washington was correct on his assessment of part of Goode's legacy.

GOODE—ON—GOODE

How does Goode view his administration? During my September 25, 1993 interview with W. Wilson Goode he said that in 1983 his strategy was to present a clear message to the people regarding the importance of his election promise which was that he was a competent manager with a proven record. Thus it was vital that he develop a media campaign structure to get the Black voter turnout that would equal the White voter turnout.

Goode says, "The media was extraordinarily fair and bent over backwards to be supportive of me. I think it was because they really wanted to see an African American win. It took a long time to get an African American mayor and I felt an absolute historical responsibility. I felt that I was carrying on my shoulders all the struggles of my ancestors for all of those years and there was no way I was going to give up. If they didn't give up in slavery, after reconstruction, why should I?"[29]

He added "I wanted Black people to feel pride."[30] "I think government, for those who are interested in people is the best place to use their talents and skills."[31]

Goode credits his 1987 campaign manager, Reynard Rouchon, with devising the winning campaign strategy that maintained the support of Blacks by investing campaign dollars to get the voters out rather than spending money on television ads. During that campaign, Goode let it be known that while he was against forced busing, he was supportive of a quality education and noted that youth unemployment was one of the city's major problems. He emphatically argued that when summer jobs for youth are provided the crime rate decreases by 20%.

The general issues for Goode were strengthening the local economy; securing cable TV for the city; beginning an anti-graffiti campaign; placing minorities and women in cabinet positions and increasing minority participation in major contracts. His situationally unique issue may be considered this; if elected he would become the city's first African American mayor in the city's 300-year history. Were the expectations and pressures high? Unbelievably so! Wilson states, "I found it to be absolutely excessive pressure. It was humbling. I knew that I can never do what they want."[32]

As a rhetorical critic one of my concerns is how effectively a message is constructed and conveyed by the speaker. In particular, how is Wilson Goode's style perceived by others?

GOODE'S SPEAKING STYLE

"Wilson Goode is not a great orator. He has a North Carolina accent, a stilted speaking style, drops his esses so agreement sounds wrong although in his head he knows what agreement is."[33] In 1983 he got his message across with the simple slogan "Will you help me?"

Local radio station W106 parodied Goode's down-home presentation of one of his speeches using his inflections of his Southern drawl and twang. However, by 1987 he had turned some of his phrases into traditional English. In the Black church he would say, "I is de Mayor and everybody gets on because I is de Mayor." Against smooth talking people like John White, Wilson never came out looking good.[34]

One of the defining moments in Goode's public speaking occurred in a debate with Frank Rizzo because he was very successful. He admitted that he trained for this particular debate; he was coached in appearance; projection; told to ignore his opponent when speaking and to not allow his opponent to seize any negative issue but to respond to issues fully.

Goode describes his personal speaking style as:

...sincere, forceful, deliberate, very unique, very distinctive voice and a combination of Southern and Philadelphian accent all mixed up together which tremendously confused people at times. For the most part I wrote my own speeches. You just can't say the words to make them sound interesting. I have a different voice for church than I do for business people and neighborhood people. I am very emotional in church, very direct. I'm very controlled in talking to business people. Free flowing, kind of rolling with the mood of the audience. However, in front of an audience I still have a degree of discomfort.[35]

From the previous information we can deduce that in an intuitive sense, Goode knew that he had to adapt to different audiences, yet the general public's impression was that he was a dull speaker. He was never viewed by anyone as an outstanding, charismatic speaker who could move an audience to action. Wilson's strength as a speaker was that he was organized. And more importantly, he was perceived as a sincere, hardworking individual who constantly referred to deeds done or to his accomplishments. By examining Goode's rhetorical image one can deduce certain trends or perceptions that may affect all African American mayors.

Cooke believes that in the 1983 campaign, neither the content of his speech nor his presentation of it mattered because the time was right for the election of Wilson Goode.

GOODE'S RHETORICAL IMAGE

Goode, the press and the citizens of Philadelphia *created* Goode's rhetorical image. What were the key elements of his image and what was in fact the reality of the perception? Table 1.1 attempts to delineate key elements of the rhetorical image/style of Wilson Goode before and after the MOVE crisis.

Table 1.1. Wilson Goode, before and after the MOVE crisis

Before MOVE	After MOVE
Hands-on, nuts-and bolts manager	A technocrat
A fair, 16-hours a day, hardworking competent leader	Incompetent leader with poor judgment
Revolutionary ideas in appointments in government of women and minorities	Co-opted by the system, top level appointments, not middle managers
Improving the economy and the skyline	Minority communities not helped as much as Center City
Level the playing field	No Black agenda
First African American mayor in 300 years	No successor in near future
Man of the future	Too close to the past
An attempt to transcend race	Race is always present
Sensitive to needs of Black community	Surrendering of interests for broader community

By studying the mayoral campaigns of African Americans, it becomes clear that there are several barriers that should be considered when determining whether or not the campaigns waged were or were not successful. The following lists a number of factors that may define challenges for future Black mayoral candidates.

CHALLENGES FOR BLACK MAYORAL CANDIDATES

1. Perceived as special-interest candidates for Blacks only or minorities.
2. If more than one African American enters the race, the issue of one of the candidates dropping out to preserve unity stays in the forefront of the campaign (1991- Philadelphia Mayoral Campaign).
3. Must always demonstrate the ability to help all citizens sometimes to the detriment of Blacks.
4. The miracle-worker, superman image is prevalent; Cities are usually in decay after years of neglect yet immediate turnaround of economy is expected.
5. The competence and credibility question is always a factor.
6. Class issues for Black candidates may become intrusive.
7. Coalitions are more difficult to hold together when trying to expand the base.
8. Media coverage is vastly different for African Americans (Black press is still important).
9. Race is always an issue.
10. Black voter education does not always translate into an organized, sustaining structure for future election of black officials.

When dealing effectively with these issues an African American mayoral candidate may have a successful bid for office.

According to Russell Cooke, "Mr. Goode's talents will serve him better as ex-Mayor. He's going to be our Jimmy Carter. Goode will always be special for Black Philadelphians."[36]

"Black officials do make a difference and they can have a positive impact on a city. Unfortunately, race will always be a factor and 75% of White people in the city will never vote for a Black person. We have to work on a whole new generation, because, I think that it is too late for this one."[37]

Although a less than optimistic view, given the current events in local politics, this assessment has more merit than one would like to acknowledge—even with the hard fought re-election of John Street or the recent election of Mayor Michael A. Nutter.

In this chapter, I have discussed the importance of studying Black mayors and the rhetorical image of W. Wilson Goode as illuminated by the press (both White and Black) and by Goode himself. Mayor Wilson Goode can be viewed as both pioneer and technocrat. In addition, a list of barriers often encountered by African American mayoral candidates is provided.

Now, more than ever, the election of Black mayors continues to be of utmost importance for Black survival in the 21st Century. And in truth—the survival of all.

In the nearby city of Wilmington, Delaware, another African American male heard and took the challenge of running for mayor in another urban northeastern city.

NOTES

1. William E. Nelson, *Black Atlantic Politics: Dilemmas of Political Empowerment in Boston and Liverpool* (Albany, N.Y.: State University of New York Press, 2000), 54.

2. Morrison, 1987, XIV.

3. Kenneth G. Weinberg, *Black Victory: Carl Stokes and the Winning of Cleveland* (Chicago: Quadrangle Books, 1968), 240.

4. *Business Week*, (December 1970): 46.

5. Lloyd F. Bitzer, "The Rhetorical Situation," *Philosophy and Rhetoric* 1, No.1 (Winter 1968): 6.

6. Robert Mullen, *Black Communications* (Washington, D.C.: University Press of America, 1982).

7. Gerard A. Hauser, *Introduction to Rhetorical Theory* (New York: Harper & Row, 1986), 3.

8. Russell Cooke, *Philadelphia Inquirer*, 1992, C4.

9. Wilson W. Goode, (with Joann Stevens) *In Goode Faith* (Valley Forge, PA: Judson Press, 1992), 189.

10. Hizkias Assefa and Paul Wahrhaftig, *Extremist Groups and Conflict Resolution: The MOVE Crisis in Philadelphia*, (New York: Praeger Publishers, 1988), 10, 22, 116.

11. Russell Cooke, *Philadelphia Inquirer*, 1992, C4.

12. Russell Cooke, Interview recorded on audio tape by Deborah F. Atwater. October 1, 1993, Philadelphia, Pennsylvania.

13. Russell Cooke, Interview.

14. Russell Cooke, Interview.

15. Russell Cooke, Interview.

16. Wilson W. Goode, (with Joann Stevens) *In Goode Faith* (Valley Forge, PA: Judson Press, 1992), 189.

17. Gayle K. Berardi, and Thomas W. Segady. "The Development of African American Newspapers in the American West: A Sociohistorical Perspective." *Journal of Negro History 75* (Summer/Fall 1990): 96.

18. Phyllis Kaniss, *The Media and the Mayor's Race: The Failure of Urban Political Reporting* (Bloomington, Indiana: Indiana University Press, 1995), 63.

19. Kaniss, *The Media and the Mayor's Race*, 100.

20. Linn Washington, Interview recorded on audio tape by Deborah F. Atwater, September 29, 1993, Philadelphia, Pennsylvania.

21. Linn Washington, Interview.

22. Linn Washington, Interview.

23. Wilson W. Goode, Personal interview, recorded on audio tape by Deborah F. Atwater, September 25, 1993.

24. Linn Washington, Interview.

25. Wilson W. Goode, Interview.

26. Russell Cooke, Interview.

27. Linn Washington, Interview.

28. Linn Washington, Interview.

29. Wilson W. Goode, Interview.

30. Wilson W. Goode, Interview.

31. *Black Enterprise*. February 1982.

32. Wilson W. Goode, Interview.

33. Russell Cooke, Interview.

34. Linn Washington, Interview.

35. Wilson W. Goode, Interview.

36. Russell Cooke, Interview.

37. Wilson W. Goode, Interview.

Chapter Two

James Sills, Jr.:
Mayor as Educator,
Wilmington, DE

Tonight we have finally come of political age and this is only the begin-
ning. We won because we believed in each other, and trusted each other.
It was a coalition of voters because of a commonality of needs. Our
campaign workers out-hustled and out-smarted our opponents. The entire
community won.

Jim Sills on the night of his election as the first
African-American Mayor of Wilmington.[1]

However, Cris Barrish of the *Delaware News Journal* describes the Sills
coalition as being 85% Blacks; wealthy Whites; some Poles; Irish and Ital-
ians.[2]

Although in close proximity to the city of Philadelphia, Jim Sills' story
varies from that of former Mayor Wilson Goode. The following is a brief
synopsis of the life and experiences of the Honorable James H. Sills, Jr.

After he was sworn in on November 3, 1992, Mayor Sills took his time to
thank everyone in attendance, even thanking Walt, the owner of Walt's Fla-
vor Crisp in Northeast Wilmington for providing his famous chicken to the
campaign volunteers and workers. Latin Americans and middle-and working
class Whites from the East side were in the audience. Sills had been considered the underdog in the Democratic primary so it was his night to savor. And
to many people, his come-from-behind, grass-roots, under-funded campaign
to unseat the two-term incumbent party-backed Dan Frawley was truly un-
expected and stunning. Frawley's base was in the traditional Irish neighborhoods of the city's West side. Even though the Wilmington population of
71,000 is over fifty per cent African-American, this was the first time that
the citizens could even have dreamed of a Sills election. Despite the fact that

Sills was well qualified by education, experience, and character, the pundits had predicted Frawley as the winner.

On September 12, Sills began his march to the office of the Mayor by defeating Frawley in the Democratic Primary. Because Republicans had not been a factor in Wilmington's Mayoral race for almost two decades, simply winning the primary practically assured Sills the victory in the general election. Everything looked good. But there was one interesting turn of events. In the general election, Sills would be running against the first African American woman—community activist Beatrice Patton Carroll who was running on a third party ticket called "A Delaware Party." This caused concern in the African American community as her candidacy created the potential of splitting the vote and dividing the unity that Sills had fought so hard to achieve in the Democratic primary election against Frawley. His rhetorical challenge was getting the voters to vote for him while trying not to say anything negative about his rival—an African American woman. But is this not a democracy in which everyone has the right to run for office?

A native of Wilmington, Beatrice Patton Carroll's family had lived in Wilmington for more than a century. She had attended Howard High School, Howard University and the University of Pennsylvania's School of Law. And she was a formidable opponent.

Carroll's extensive and impressive community and civic involvements and activities included Vice Chairman, Coalition to Save Our Children; Board of Directors, Howard High School Alumni Association; Chairman, Board of Directors Walnut Street Branch YMCA; Chairman, Delaware Adult Entertainment Establishment's Commission; Member, American Cancer Society; Board of Directors, People's Settlement Association Credit Union; Board of Directors, Minority Business Association of Delaware; Founding Member, Friends of Wilmington and Charter Member, Brandywine Professional Association.

Throughout her adult life, Bea Carroll's leadership, dedication and commitment to the residents of Wilmington, New Castle County and the State of Delaware had earned her the praise of several community groups and institutions. As Administrative Assistant to the President of New Castle County Council, Carroll had firsthand experience in the management and operation of government. In that capacity she annually prepared the operating budget for the Council, managed the Council staff and facilitated the Council's annual review of the countywide operating and capital budgets. She worked in large corporations and NGOs and owned her own small business. Bea Carroll had fought all of her life to serve Delaware and bring about change.

Carroll's campaign issues were four previous years of budget deficits; excessively high under and unemployment rates; escalating substandard housing conditions and rising homelessness among women and men with children. Putting Wilmingtonians back to work was one of her top priorities. Carroll planned to tackle the problems of bureaucracy that always faces an elected official by "not going along to get along."[3]

But why would she want to run for Mayor at this particular time, given one of her opponents was an African American male? Politics has always been part game; a game of promises—and primarily a man's game. When smiling, handshaking, seasoned politicians are elected, the favors are handed out to their associates—not to the people who elected them. Bea Carroll concluded, "I do not need to join the good ole' boys. Being a part of seven generations, I am deeply rooted in Wilmington, I know what Wilmingtonians want."[4] Being a woman of strength and character, she believed that she had more to offer than the men who were running for office. She was not a part of the club and that was fine with her.

Nevertheless, her qualifications and her life-long connections to the community were not enough to win the election. On November 3, Sills beat Carroll, 20,700 to 2,160 votes respectively. After his narrow margin of victory over Frawley in the Democratic primary, Sills campaigned hard, knowing that he needed every vote he could get. (Sills beat Frawley by 925 votes which was 54% of the vote in that election.)

Prior to his election, Cris Barrish of the *Wilmington News Journal,* one of the few in the media who felt that Sills had a good chance of winning the election said, "I viewed Sills as a serious threat."[5]

SILLS' SPEAKING STYLE

Barrish describes Sills' speaking style as, "Respectful, stumbles at times, speaks like a professor, private, aloof, but he does get his message across."[6] To Dan Frawley's lament, he apparently did not take Sills seriously. Frawley raised three times the money that Sills did for the general election campaign some $90,000 plus to Sills' $32,000 most of which came from Bob Watson's Insurance agency, small businesses, churches and individuals."[7] In fact, $9,000 came from Mayor Sills' own funds.

JIM SILLS-THE MAN

Many were asking, *Who is this Black Populist Moses and what do we really know about him?* Some even felt that he did not have enough experience as an administrator to handle the city's budget of $100 million dollars. But during his term in office he proved them wrong.

Sills lived in Raleigh, North Carolina until he was ten. Mayor Sills came from humble beginnings, but he became a soldier; social worker; community firebrand; legislator; academician and a dedicated husband and father.

In 1958 Sills came to Wilmington as a young social worker to do a six-month internship in the Delaware Family Court. He moved to Delaware to accept a position in the Delaware Family Court after earning his degree and completing his internship at Atlanta University.

He was born in Raleigh, North Carolina and grew up on his parent's farm in Louisburg. For three years, he lived in the Chavis Heights Public Housing Development. His mother, Marjorie Shaw earned a degree from Shaw University in Raleigh while working as secretary to the President of Shaw. She was in the American Red Cross and lived overseas in London. His parents were divorced when he was ten years old. When his mother found a job as a social worker and moved to Philadelphia, Sills lived with his father for four years.

While in Raleigh in the 30s and 40s, Sills was exposed to racial discrimination. At that time, his father was the headwaiter at S&W Cafeteria. Sills relates an incident that happened to him while he and his father were walking down the streets of Raleigh: A White man was walking toward them, and as he approached them the man yelled "N-----" and demanded that they get off the sidewalk and walk in the street. Sills never forgot that incident and believes that it has had a significant impact on the way he approaches racial relations and equitable treatment for all.

For a time, he lived on the farm with his grandparents and worked hard picking cotton and helping with the farm work. Those who know him know that he is no stranger to hard work, often putting in long hours. At fourteen, he went to Raleigh and lived with his father at the local YMCA. He worked as a part-time waiter but quickly learned that he could make more money hanging out at the local pool hall. Playing hooky from school resulted in his failing of the eleventh grade. When his mother found out about it, she took immediate custody of her son and sent him to Palmer Memorial Institute in Sedalia, North Carolina, a Black boarding school where he finished high school. After graduating, when he contemplated entering the Navy, his mother interceded again. This intervention changed his life.

After Marjorie Sills attended an event where Dr. Benjamin Mays (then President of Morehouse College in Atlanta) spoke, she was determined to send Jim to Morehouse. On a regular basis Jim Sills heard Dr. Mays reiterate, "Young Black men should take on responsibility through public service and personal example to be a positive change in their communities." And he never forgot those words which would help shape his destiny in public service. His strong religious convictions are evidenced by his position as Elder at Wilmington's Presbyterian Church of Our Savior. Dr. Mays, his mother and countless others including his professors at Morehouse, convinced him that one could, with proper education, determination, and a strong belief in one's self, achieve and prosper. After earning his Bachelor of Arts degree in Political Science he spent two years in the Army's Military Police, serving one year in Germany and one year in Kentucky. In the early 1960s, he became a community activist in Wilmington, an activity that would later lead to his appointment as Director of Peoples' Settlement House from 1962-1967.

Following the assassination of Martin Luther King, Jr. in 1968, as a result of his high visibility job as Director of Peoples' Settlement House, he spent a lot of time on the streets talking and working with the people, advocating his philosophy of moderation and conciliation over confrontation and violence. In 1983, he became a representative of the East Side in the General Assembly. Following the riots he became the Director of the newly formed Association of Greater Wilmington Neighborhood Centers and became the first African American to win an At-Large position on Wilmington's City Council.

He became more familiar with Wilmington while serving as Executive Director of the now-defunct Association of Greater Wilmington's Neighborhood Centers. He earned a Master's degree at Atlanta University before he came to Wilmington. In October 1969 (before it became a rallying cry for some in national politics) Sills said the following about family values, "Many of the problems of the inner city begin with the families themselves. Not enough is being done by Wilmington social agencies to help stabilize families. One problem in Wilmington is that there are no broad, overall goals toward which the community is working."[8] It was always Jim's desire that his wife, Evelyn stay at home with their three children because he believed that it was one way to stabilize his family. Unfortunately, his wife, Evelyn passed away in June of 2006.

At the time of this interview (1993), his oldest child, Jim III was Vice President of the Tuskegee Bank in Alabama. His other son, Mark was an Assistant Coach of basketball at Howard High School, Wilmington, Delaware and his daughter Julie was a Sales Representative for the DuPont Company in Cleveland. He and his wife have four grandchildren and over the years they provided a positive family role-model for the community.

Upon hearing a speech he delivered at the National Conference on Social Welfare in June 1970, Whitney Young, former Civil Rights leader commented "Wilmington is fortunate to have such fine black leadership."[9]

In 1972 he lost his bid for City Council President to Frank Vari, mainly due to Vari's solid support in the Italian and White areas of the city. However, this would be the last race that Sills would lose. Vari later lost to Frawley who subsequently became Mayor. Vari says of Sills, "Neither of us said anything against the other. We both ran clean campaigns. I've always considered Jim a good friend."[10]

Using his connection with the University of Delaware, Sills convinced Harold Brown to establish an Urban Agent office in downtown Wilmington to address social and economic problems. In 1974 Sills began working part-time on his Ph.D. in Social Work and Social Research at Bryn Mawr College, and completed his degree in 1981.

To his credit as a community servant, Sills was a member and past President of the Christiana School District and served as President of the Wilmington Branch of the NAACP. In 1983, as a State Representative he had the chance to regularly express his views on social and family services. He was the principal founder and Chairperson from 1987-1993 of the Delaware Community Reinvestment Action Council. He successfully convinced Delaware Trust, Bank of Delaware and Wilmington Savings Fund Society to provide minorities with low income housing and small business loans. Specifically $50 million was made available to low-income communities in Delaware, $10 million per year. The Delaware Community Reinvestment Action Council also negotiated with the banks to hire credit counselors and have assistant managers in neighborhood centers that had the authority to approve loans up to $10,000 and to change the loan minimum requirement from $5,000 to $1500. Clearly, Sills was dedicated to making improvements to the city which would benefit all of its citizens.

HIS VISION FOR THE CITY OF WILMINGTON

Following the historic Wilmington election, Sills said:

> I inherited a city that had and still does have some serious financial problems. They're not critical, and I don't believe that it can be compared to some of the financial problems of some of the surrounding cities are having. We have ended the last two years before I took office with deficits, cumulative deficits of close to $11 million. Our cost of services has gone up 4.8% over the last five years and income only up 2.5%. So the last two years before I came into office we had used reserves to cover those deficits for those two fiscal years. So we have had some serious financial problems but they weren't critical and they still aren't critical. We have a thriving port. The previous administration was successful

and I've had some success as well in getting business from the Philadelphia port, but because of the labor problems up there, a number of companies have chosen to come here. I'd have to say too, that I have inherited a city which has a well organized corporate community, organized in that they have been heavily involved in public policy matters in part reflected in the fact that they got a disproportionate amount of city resources. But they were there and had established a relationship with the city which is healthy and which I capitalized on. And I said if you elect me we've got to establish a downtown development corporation, a nonprofit downtown development corporation to help revitalize our central downtown business district. I made a lot about the importance of forming public private partnership and as a result, we have established something called Wilmington 2000, a nonprofit development corporation which is heavily supported by the large corporations.[11]

After his election many wondered how he would govern such a diverse and problem-wracked city. His vision of a "new-spirit," "new commitment," and a "new city," however, won him the election. His call to voters "Challenge your mind to change your world," was taken from his January 5th letter to the citizens in the official *Sills Inaugural Souvenir Booklet.* (1993) Sills advocates the following:

1. There needs to be better cooperation between the governments of Wilmington and New Castle County. County areas outside of the city need to be more open to low-and-middle income housing to help ease overcrowding in various city areas.
2. City government should be more representative in terms of personnel of the population in general.[12]
   "White males have dominated city government and we need more managers and workers to make us more representative of the city population as a whole."[13]
3. The Mayor and the city government should improve the quality of life for every citizen and address social problems like unemployment, insufficient and substandard housing and drug abuse.[14]

Sills won the election in part because he knocked on one third of the doors of the homes in Wilmington from 9:00 AM to 6:00 PM asking for people to vote for him. Of his many positive traits; most notably, he is a hard worker, often putting in long hours, seven days a week.

In his private life he likes freshwater fishing, although he says there isn't much time for it. He is an avid reader and he keeps a note pad at his side so that when he wakes up he can write any ideas that come to him. His wife Evelyn says that he has no ego problems. According to Steve Piquet, director of the College of Urban Affairs and Public Policy's Urban Agent Division at the University of Delaware.[15] "He is honest, has integrity, determination, intelligence and mental toughness, as well as a genuine concern for people."[16] "He is a bottoms-up leader and he has built his reputation on one-to-one re-lationships."[17]

However, there are those who feel that Sills' penchant for slow, deliber-ate evaluations before making important decisions became a hindrance. In response, Sills said:

> I'm deliberate when I make a decision, I don't know that I'm slow. I try to gather facts, it's part of my background. I don't apologize, but I think that's good. On the other hand, I've been in office now and I've made some tough decisions and I've had to make them quickly, because they needed to be made quickly, and I didn't have good information. Sometimes you've got to rely upon your gut, you know, to make a decision. So deliberate, yes, and analytical, yes, and I don't apologize for that.[18]

His wife Evelyn believed that her husband sometimes trusts people a little too much, but at that time said that thus far it hasn't backfired. When asked if he is indeed too trusting, Sills remarks, "It hasn't been a problem over my many years of leadership. I do tend to trust people; I tend to want to give people the benefit of the doubt. But I think it's helped to attract a constituency and stabilize a constituency."[19] His record as a community worker, educator and legislator clearly demonstrates his ability to interact positively with all segments of the Wilmington community. He put together one of the most racially and ethnically mixed, blue-chip administrative transition teams in Wilmington's history.

Both Allen Rusten (nationally recognized expert in state and local gov-ernments) and Dave Swayze (Wilmington law firm of Duane, Morris and Hecksher and Board member of New Castle County Economic Development Corporation) agreed that he came into office during a most difficult financial crunch period of an ongoing recession which made it difficult to get new programs approved because the government was functioning on a bare-bones budget. Upon taking office Sills faced a revenue deficit of $11 million dol-lars and thus had little choice but to raise taxes immediately. In addition, four public employees' contracts (police, firefighters and white collar workers) had to be skillfully negotiated. And he had to decide what to do about a $47.5 million dollar convention center.

Peuquet says that "There is no black agenda. Issues that concern African Americans affect all—economy, education, and the quality of life."[20] Sills echoed this sentiment saying:

I felt that Wilmington needed a mayor who could be a good listener who would use his or her office to give people hope. We give people hope by being an advocate for change and saying, taking public positions that let them know that you identify with problems of sexism and ageism and racism and elderly discrimination. I also said that I thought that I was concerned with the fact that at the time I was running [for] 22,000 people under the age of 18 were not registered to vote, the vast minority of them were people located in largely black areas, and that I wanted to be the kind of mayor that would lead more people and minority people. And I was pretty clear about that, to have some incentive as a result of my election to get involved in the political process.[21]

SILLS AND THE MAINSTREAM PRESS

When asked how the media treated him during his campaign Sills responded:

I don't think that I was treated fair. They really didn't think that I would win. They really didn't feel I would win, that was obvious from the beginning. I think my coverage is getting better. I got off to a rocky start, but not because of the news journals [as] much more with the city council the first couple of months. But that seems to have been resolved. I've got a good working relationship with city council and the paper. The coverage has been good in part because they've seen evidence of my support from the business community.[22]

At the end of the year, the Mayor's office and the newspaper sponsored a New Year's Eve program downtown called "First Night" which was an event geared to family-oriented activities.

After seven months, the paper did a feature article on Sills. When referring to this article Sills says:

Those kinds of comparisons in this country given the history of racism are probably inevitable. It's not fair, but it's inevitable that papers are going to have higher standards because you are black, the first black. I did complain to the editorial board that [after] just three to four months, that they were examining me more closely than they had examined previous mayors. There were articles written about every little thing I said. I complained that I felt that I was being unduly scrutinized and I felt that there was some racial motive to that. And White folks are uncomfortable with differences, and they fear many differences. And they tend to overreact to difference. That's a problem that newspaper reporters have just like anybody else. The publisher of the paper agreed with some of my criticisms where they found that the reporters had started with editorializing an event before stating the facts.[23]

The News Journal put him under a microscope. They were waiting for him
to trip and fall, every hiccup, every ah he said in his words. They were not
objective in their reporting. It clearly shows in their coverage of what he did
and it still does show in the way they depict him now.[24] This perspective is
shared by Hanifa Shabazz of *Drumbeat*, African American Newspaper, Interview, October 25, 1993.

SILLS AND THE BLACK PRESS

At one point in his campaign, Sills was referred to as a Black popular Moses,
to which Sills replied, "I don't know about the Moses bit, but I certainly had
a grassroots campaign."[25] Mayor Sills knew in advance that the Black min-
isters supported him, which was important because in the past there had not
been much support for Black candidates. According to Hanifa Shabazz, the
campaign centered on the need for a mayor who was sensitive to the needs
of the entire community. Yes—he was a Black mayor, but he did things that
were beneficial not only for the Black community, but that were beneficial
for all communities.

Noting that conditions in Wilmington had deteriorated during the past ten
years, Shabazz said "I think he inherited a city that was in distress. Everyone
was looking for him to do a miracle turnaround but there was so much disease
that had to be cut away and restructured, built, that it was going to take some
time."[26] "A Black mayor can be perceived and seen by the Black community
and Black voters as more objective than a White mayor. The White mayor
only sees one way. A Black mayor see, he's more sensitive to all people than
the White mayor. The White mayor only sees one side."[27]

In regard to the campaign, the *Drumbeat* "depicted his campaign and him
as well as the way we do our general reporting. If there was something negative about his campaign, we quoted that as well as his positives. The *Drumbeat* is a newspaper, for, to, and about the African American community so
his campaign was definitely one of the highlights for our community."[28]

SILLS SPEAKING STYLE

Hanifah Shabazz characterizes Sills' speaking style this way:

> Mayor Sills is not a great orator. And because of his not being a great orator,
> he has to assure that what he says is strong that you can overlook the plausible
> presentation. When he was on the board at these meetings we would discuss
> very technical things and he listens, you can tell he listens strongly to what's

being said and I think because he has so much on his mind sometimes it kind of distracts him from being the orator that he can be. But even though he might not be a great orator, his points are great and direct and so he still gets his points across. He might not get your emotions all up, but he leaves you with a point of thought as to what he was saying.[29]

Describing his speaking style, Sills said:

It's related to my personality. I'm by nature reserved and private. I'm not, when I speak. I generally have an outline, very deliberate. I've gotten better at being spontaneous, but that doesn't come naturally to me. I'm a lot more emotional when I'm talking to low income/minority groups and that's because I think that I have to be in order to reach them. I'm a lot more deliberative and analytic when I speak to white groups. I think I've been generally effective in communicating to both groups. I see myself as a good public speaker, not excellent, but well. I consider myself to be very knowledgeable, but I'm not the kind of extemporaneous speaker that I'd like to be. I don't know that I'll ever be. I'll tell you that one of the reasons that I won this election, at least some people tell me, not some but a lot, was because of the debates. We had four debates and, maybe a lot were surprised at how well I did at the debates, because my opponent was a lawyer (Frawley), a guy with a gift of gab, very comfortable speaking. But I came across as serious which I happen to be. I came across as knowledgeable, which I happen to be. I'm told I did a very good job.[30]

BUILDING A COALITION

When asked about Mayor Sills' coalition, Hanifa Shabazz was quick to say the following:

He has a coalition of people who are supportive of him through his political period as well as people who were fed up with the other political engine. And his coalition is a mixture of all types of people, progressive people who want to make some things change. He has an old generation as well as a younger generation. It's a mixture because he won strong in some of the White areas as well as Hispanic areas as well as the Asian areas. His votership wasn't just one sided, all Black. He had a strong following. Like, I said, the city was in great disaster. I believe this last election pulled out the Hispanics to vote more than they ever have.[31]

In response to the question "Do Black mayors make a difference?" Mayor Sills responded:

I think the answer is yes. We have to use our positions to help more low income people and Blacks in particular to feel greater ownership of government, to have more initiative to be involved, to be inspired by our presence, our leadership, and seeing our ability to manage like anybody else, removing some of the myths about blacks [not] being able to manage. So I think Blacks should feel more comfortable utilizing the political process. It's critically important in a city's ability to be able to attract resources outside of itself.

I've given a lot of speeches and I've encouraged kids to go to college because they need certain educational and technical skills in order to be economically independent and take care of a family. Begin now [to] become a city council-man, run for governor, to being president. That black professionals in particular have a role and a responsibility for leadership and public service that goes back to Booker T. Washington, and Mary McCloud Bethune... We don't have rich white descendants that come and provide public service free, and black professionals are expected to do that. The real challenge, one of the major challenges facing mayors of any city, but especially black mayors, is using his leadership to unleash the creative energies of people, especially in self-help programs and especially in community development activities and community development corporation activities."[32]

Mayor Sills faced general issues common to all mid-to-large cities. However, his situationally unique issues involved a press that did not take him seriously as a viable candidate in his bid to become the first Black mayor of Wilmington, and he received heavy scrutiny because of his status as the first Black mayor of Wilmington, Delaware.

Sills was a member of the University of Delaware faculty from 1972-1997 and was on leave from the university during his first term as mayor. He retired from the University after his reelection in 1997. In March of 2001 a $250,000 scholarship fund was established at the University of Delaware by Wilmington business and corporate groups and friends of James H. Sills, Jr. A stipend award is presented annually to a graduate student in the School of Urban Affairs and Public Policy in the College of Human Services Education and Public Policy.

When asked by me about his administration on September 18, 2009, Mayor Sills said that he had some sense of accomplishment, but also there were disappointments and challenges. He was successful in reducing the size and cost of city government, more businesses and corporations relocated to the city and there was more economic development along the waterfront, however, he was challenged by the fact that there was more crime and there was not a significant change in the quality of life for all of the citizens of Wilmington.

Like other Black mayors, James Sills inherited a city that was plagued with numerous problems and resource limitations. Yet Sills, as "Mayor as Educator", was able to use his educational skills of organization, articulation and perseverance to build a coalition of multi-ethnic groups in the city of

Wilmington. His previous community positions and life experiences helped him to become the first Black Mayor of Wilmington.

South of Wilmington, Delaware, in our Nation's capital, another story was unfolding. An historic story that provided an opportunity for an African American woman to lead a large urban city.

NOTES

1. Charles P.Wilson (1993). Wilmington under Sills. *Delaware Today*, January, 28.
2. Cris Barrish, (1993) *Delaware News Journal*. Personal interview. (recorded on audio tape by Deborah F. Atwater), October 27, 1993.
3. M. L. Morris. (1992 October). "To Bea of Not To Bea? That is the Question," *Drumbeat,* 11.
4. M. L. Morris. (1992 October). "To Bea of Not To Bea? That is the Question," *Drumbeat,* 11.
5. Cris Barrish (1993) *Delaware News Journal*. Personal interview. (recorded on audio tape)October 27, 1993.
6. Cris Barrish, interview, (10/27/93).
7. M. L. Morris, *Drumbeat* (October, 1992).
8. Charles P. Wilson (1993). Wilmington under Sills. *Delaware Today*, 30.
9. Charles P. Wilson, *Delaware Today*, 48.
10. Charles P. Wilson, *Delaware Today*, 48.
11. James H. Sills. (1993). Personal interview. (Recorded on audiotape). 21 October.
12. James H. Sills (1993). *Wilmington: A New Spirit: A New Commitment:* Inaugural Ceremony. 5 January- Official Inaugural Souvenir Booklet.
13. Charles P. Wilson, *Delaware Today*, 30.
14. *Wilmington: A New Spirit: A New Commitment*: Inaugural Ceremony. 5 January- Official Inaugural Souvenir Booklet.
15. Charles P. Wilson, *Delaware Today*, 31.
16. Charles P. Wilson, *Delaware Today*, 31.
17. Charles P. Wilson, *Delaware Today*, 31.
18. James H. Sills. (1993). Personal interview. (Recorded on audiotape). 21 October.
19. James H. Sills. (1993). Personal interview. (Recorded on audiotape). 21 October.
20. Charles P. Wilson, *Delaware Today*, 41.
21. James H. Sills. (1993). Personal interview. (Recorded on audiotape). 21 October.
22. James H. Sills. (1993). Personal interview. (Recorded on audiotape). 21 October.

23. James H. Sills, Interview.

24. Hanifah Shabazz, (1993) Personal interview. (Recorded on audiotape). 25 October.

25. James H. Sills, Interview.

26. Hanifah Shabazz, Interview.

27. Hanifah Shabazz, (1993) Personal interview.

28. Hanifah Shabazz, Interview.

29. Hanifah Shabazz Interview.

30. James H. Sills, Interview.

31. Hanifah Shabazz, Interview.

32. James H. Sills, Interview.

Chapter Three

Sharon Pratt Dixon Kelly:
African American Woman Reformer,
Mayor, Washington, DC

In another urban setting a call for action was heard and met by an African American woman, Sharon Pratt Dixon Kelly. Sharon Pratt Kelly, former mayor of Washington, D.C., was born Sharon Pratt, in Washington, D.C. on Jan 30, 1944, elder child of Carlisle Pratt, a Superior Court judge, and Mildred Petticord. When Sharon was four years old her mother died of cancer. With her younger sister, Benaree and their father, she went to live with her paternal grandmother and aunt in Washington, D.C. Later when her father remarried, Sharon lived with him and her stepmother. She attended Gage and Rudolph Elementary Schools and McFarland Junior High School and graduated with honors from Roosevelt High School in Washington, D.C. in 1961. In 1965 she received a BA in Political Science with honors from Howard University, Washington D.C., and three years later graduated from Howard's Law School with a JD degree. While in law school she married her first husband, former D.C. council member Arrington Dixon with whom she had two daughters, Aimee Arrington and Drew Arrington Dixon. The couple divorced in 1982. In 1972, she became a Professor of Law at the Antioch School of Law in Washington, D.C., a post she held for four years.[1]

Kelly began her legal career in 1970 as House Counsel for the Joint Center for Political Studies in Washington, D.C., before entering private law practice with the legal firm of Pratt and Queen in 1971 where she focused on the rights of children in custodial cases, provided legal representation for juveniles and became a leader in the emerging area of family rights law. In 1972 former Speaker of the House Thomas "Tip" O'Neil appointed her to be Vice Chairman of the District of Columbia's Law Revision Commission which transferred the city's criminal code from Congress to the District. From 1972 to 1976 she taught business law at the Antioch School of Law in Washington, D.C., reaching the rank of Full Professor. After leaving Antioch School of Law she served as a member of the General Counsel's Office at Potomac Electric Power Company (PEPCO) from 1976 to 1979 and was appointed Director of Consumer Affairs. In 1986 PEPCO, the Washington area power utility, appointed her as its first female Vice President for Public Policy where she worked to develop programs to assist low- and fixed-income residents of the District of Columbia.[2]

While representing Washington D.C., Kelly (1977 to 1990) was elected Treasurer of the Democratic National Committee, serving from 1985 to 1989. Her close ties to the national Democratic Party furthered her local ambitions. She launched her mayoral campaign with a lavish, well-attended party during the 1988 Democratic National Convention in Atlanta, Georgia.

The Washington Times April 17, 1990 edition described a day in the campaign of candidate Sharon Pratt Dixon Kelly thusly:

> The assembly looked like a Baptist church revival-people nodding their heads in affirmation while speaking in preacher-like fashion, one hand on her hip and the other jabbing the air, railed against the ills of D. C. government. She was telling the senior citizens meeting that she wanted to cut a deal: elect her as mayor and witness the abolition of 2,000 mid- management jobs, among other things.[3]

On November 6, 1990, defying the odds, Kelly became the first African American woman elected mayor of Washington, D.C., with a landside 86 percent of the vote, becoming the first African-American woman to serve as executive of a major American city. Candidate Dixon won by attacking Mayor Marion Barry and portraying herself as an outsider despite her long experience in the national Democratic Party as treasurer and committeewoman.[4] However, she soon discovered that "Much as Wilson Goode in Philadelphia and David Dinkins in New York have learned before, Dixon will find that the lack of money for city programs can stifle the best of campaign pledges."[5]

Commentators credited Kelly's mayoral victory to her demonstrated commitment to the D.C. community which spanned more than twenty years. With her positive campaign slogan of "Yes, We Will," Kelly promised voters an "honest deal" that would restore the city to greatness and improve the quality of life for all of its people. She stunned observers when she promised to fire two thousand midlevel managers immediately, and many citizens were impressed with her eloquence and by the fact that she was an "outsider" with no apparent entanglements in local politics. Most importantly, she was not an ally of her predecessor, Mayor, Marion S. Barry Jr. Barry's first four years could be considered successful. But his last two terms prior to Kelly's election were marred by continuous scandals, cronyism and mismanagement. Kelly inherited an accumulated deficit of $331 million and a severe cash shortage.

In 1978 Barry inherited a government that was already oversized and under managed. After nearly twelve years in office, having failed to address those problems and having been convicted of Federal charges of cocaine possession, he chose not to run for reelection in 1990. Barry's downfall produced an upsurge of support for reforming the District's government. And Kelly, with her promise to "clean house" along with her endorsement by the highly respected *Washington Post*, rode the resulting political mood to easy victories in the September Democratic primary and the November general election.

It is generally acknowledged that Washington is overwhelmingly Democratic and that Barry had developed his own coalition of public employee unions and big real estate developers. But Barry's downfall produced a surge for reform, the beneficiary of which was Sharon Pratt Kelly. Kelly began by winning the 1990 September Democratic primary with 35%[6] versus 25% of the vote for Councilman John Ray and 21% of the vote for Councilwoman Charlene Drew Jarvis.[7]

Solving the District of Columbia's countless problems would not be as easy as winning the election. The bureaucracy was regarded by many as indifferent to the citizens it was designed to serve. Like other urban areas, the District of Columbia had a multitude of problems including an underfinanced and weak public school system; urban economic decay; high unemployment; drug trafficking and homelessness. But even more disturbing was the financial crisis that had resulted in the city's $300 million dollar deficit at the end of the 1990 fiscal year. Faced with an estimated city budget gap of $750 million over the coming 18 months, Mayor Sharon Pratt Kelly proposed eliminating 2,659 government positions and raising $50 million in new taxes and argued that a comprehensive overhaul of city government was needed. As the city's manager, the U.S. Congress, appropriated $100 million in Congressional Emergency Funding for the following fiscal year.

Initially, Kelly seemed determined to downsize government and inaugurated programs aimed at restructuring the bureaucracy by automation and retraining. She reduced the number of city employees by 2,000 through attrition and retirements. However, fewer than 200 workers were actually fired and not replaced. These changes were neither broad nor deep enough to close the gap between the District's income and outflow. To effect many of her reforms, Kelly forged public-private partnerships, encouraged area businesses to use their ingenuity to help develop programs that would serve and help save the city's young, middle-aged, seniors and deprived citizens. These partnerships helped to foster more jobs and encouraged international trade ventures.

Under the Kelly administration the police were more involved in the neighborhoods and built a citizen network in the form of neighborhood patrol groups and community gun-turn-in projects. She also strengthened the police-training program and the communications system of the police department. There were also stronger partnerships with the Prince George's County Police of Maryland's State Police. Every category of crime in the District of Columbia declined during her term as mayor.

On a personal level, Kelly's first year was traumatic. Her grandmother died. And a trusted friend and adviser died when a city ambulance went to the wrong address. James Kelly, a businessman from New York City whom she had married at the end of her first year, never seemed comfortable in the public spotlight or in the supporting role of First Spouse. The couple never had children.

Despite her successes, Sharon Kelly was never able to gain full control of the city as a whole as the bureaucrats and city council members remained loyal to Barry. Indeed, some might argue that the city as a whole was still loyal to Barry. During Kelly's second year in office, Barry backed an initiative to recall her from office. While the recall was unsuccessful, it forced Kelly to retreat from the tough reforms she had promised during her campaign. During a brief speech at Howard University, on February 3, 1994, she expressed two priorities; working with young people and the needs of senior citizens, saying that the challenges were great but not impossible to address. She also stated that there was too much bureaucracy but added, "I have a real commitment to young people. I have a tough campaign, but young people keep me going. If we love our children they will meet us more than half way. Please heed my call to action."[8] Considering that the audience was primarily college students, her speech was short but appropriate.

Kelly blamed Congress for Washington's continuing financial problems and further alienated Congress by submitting inaccurate and false information regarding the city's finances. But going in, she knew that the information was sketchy, and political observers believe that her lack of experience was a major problem for her and a possible reason for her acceptance of this false and inaccurate report and that the media's coverage of her was not very positive toward the end of her tenure in office.

Kelly's continuing criticism of Congress in regard to the city's financial woes and her support for D.C. statehood alienated potential Democratic allies who controlled Congress. Congress became alarmed by the deficit spending under Kelly and ordered her to make budget cuts, a step that increased Federal control over the city. Many believed that Kelly's actions reduced the District's powers of self-government rather than increasing them.

By 1993 she had built a palatial office for herself outside the District Building, (the formal, designated building housing the mayor's office and other district offices and agencies), and had put a makeup artist on the city payroll. Political observers increasingly saw such extravagances and her lack of political experience as major problems, prompting some disillusioned voters to encourage Marion Barry's comeback. After Barry had served six months in prison for his cocaine conviction in 1992 he was elected to the city council. In 1994 he defeated Kelly in the mayoral election.

In an August 1, 1993 appearance on Black Entertainment Television's, "Personal Diary," Sharon Pratt Kelly said that she wanted to be a good role model for her two daughters that she still believed that dreams can become real; one has to make the most of each moment and not worry about what people say.

She wanted to be remembered for three things:

1. Freed own home town, political power, statehood
2. Economic empowerment for African Americans
3. Helping our children[9]

KELLY'S AWARDS

Kelly received the 1983, NAACP Presidential Award, the 1991 Thurgood Marshall Award of Excellence and the 1986 Mary McLeod Bethune—W. E. B. Du Bois Award from the Congressional Black Caucus. She has been honored for distinguished leadership by the United Negro College Fund and was the recipient of an award for distinguished service from the Federation of Women's Clubs whose mission is to improve communities through volunteer service. Although her time in office was not as stellar as predicted or as she had hoped it would be, Sharon Pratt Dixon Kelly will be remembered as the first native of Washington, D.C. and the first African-American woman to be elected mayor of a major American city. Her platform included major reform for the city of D.C, and a clean sweep of all of the old baggage and traditions of the city. She faced the same general issues and problems of other mayors in this book, but she had *the situationally unique* issue of being an African American woman in a city that was loyal to a former African American male mayor.

Some African Americans are called to serve in a caretaker role or capacity of a city. The next mayor to be discussed answered such a call.

NOTES

1. http://www.blackpast.org/?q=aah/kelly-sharon-pratt-dixon-1944.
2. Sam Fulwood, III, "Mayor Sharon Pratt Dixon: Washington's New Hope." *Emerge*: February 1991, 37.

3. *Washington Times*, April 17, 1990.

4. Gloria Borger. "Sharon Pratt Dixon: Like Other City Leaders, D.C.'s New Boss Needs A Miracle" *U.S. News and World Report*, 31 Dec. 1990, 73.

5. Fulwood, *Emerge*, 38.

6. "A Pick With a Shovel: Promising to clean house, an anti-Barry reformer wins in D.C." *Time,* 24 September 1990:52.

7. National Journal's *The Almanac of American Politics 1996*, which was published in July of 1995, District of Columbia.

8. Sharon Pratt Kelly speech at Howard University, February 3, 1994.

9. *Black Entertainment Television: Personal Diary*: Sharon Pratt Kelly, August 1, 1993. 10:30 AM.

Chapter Four

Aaron Thompson:
Mayor as Caretaker,
Camden, NJ

When conditions make it impossible for Black mayors to make reforms they may be asked to be 'caretakers'. Mayor Aaron Thompson is one such example. In Camden, New Jersey, Mayor Aaron Thompson took the challenge of serving as a "care-taker" mayor for ten months. There are those who would argue that some current mayors are caretakers even though they have served full terms. During Mayor Thompson's tenure he encountered problems similar to those faced by Goode, Sills, and Pratt Kelly.

In 1990 when Randy Primus resigned to work for New Jersey Governor James Florio, Aaron Thompson had been a councilman for only five months when the Council and the Democratic machine appointed him as mayor. There were Council members more experienced than Thompson (some had served for thirteen years) but the party wanted Thompson. He had been involved in politics for years but had never run for office, often referring to himself as a street-level worker. The Council members assumed that he would do whatever they asked of him and sign any paper they placed before him. But he had other ideas. Because he grew up in Camden and knew and loved the city, Thompson believed that he could make a difference. But few believed in Camden, and spirits were low because of the negative images of the city, i.e., it was dubbed the "gun capital of the world," perceived to be a place where "everyone's on welfare," and "a place where no one wants to work." Ten months later he ran and won the election.

"I wanted to become Mayor, because I felt that I could do something. I'm leaving office with new housing projects and new buildings waiting to start."[1]

In 1992 an anti-arson task force was established (similar to the one in Detroit) with 1200 community volunteers on the street to help maintain order. Thompson increased the number of police during his tenure and implemented a fully automated computerized violations room. When CNN and CBS came to Camden in 1992 and Thompson took them on a tour of the city, both crews left because nothing was 'happening' that night. An ethnically diverse community of African Americans, Hispanics, and Asians, Thompson and others encouraged support for all who wanted to start a business.

One positive image of Camden was and continues to be the Campbell's Soup Company. Mayor Thompson compared its importance (as an image) to Philadelphia's Liberty Bell and the Phillies. Today, the Aquarium, the Campbell's Soup Company's International Headquarters and the Waterfront are very positive images for the city of Camden.

THOMPSON'S IMAGE

Thompson refers to himself as a college drop out who represents the people. "I have a relationship with a mass of people."[2] He was concerned that too many graduate from college and go right into politics instead of working for a while and getting some real life experience which he views as essential for being a good politician and public servant.[3]

THOMPSON ON
MAYOR WILSON GOODE AND MAYOR RANDY PRIMUS

Thompson praised Goode for his "exceptional background, he was a city manager and he has the tools for relationships on how to deal with a wide range of people. He was a fine mayor. He was a good guy. Most Black mayors when we get control of the cities, they are in need of funds and the economic base is usually controlled by Whites."[4]

As in most of the cases discussed in this book, Thompson's assessment was right on target. When Mayor Primus became the first Black mayor in 1981 the city was two days away from bankruptcy. Primus inherited a $5 million budget deficit and a declining tax base and therefore had no choice but to increase taxes. The state of New Jersey began to monitor the city's budget process which eventually led to the State taking over city finances in 2000. The city lost 60% of its base and had begun to deteriorate. However, during Primus' two-term tenure as Mayor, the important development of the Waterfront began.

THOMPSON AND THE PRESS

During his short term in office Thompson felt that he was treated fairly by the press, and stressed that he had an open door policy, "I spend my time in office, 9-5, because I'm retired. I'm just the Mayor."⁵ During our interview, Mayor Thompson said that he believes that as the city cleans up and rebuilds, many will return, influenced in part by the number of positive stories covered by the media.

THOMPSON'S ADVICE TO FUTURE AFRICAN AMERICAN POLITICIANS: TRANSPARENCY AND INTEGRITY

"I am open and honest. You can ask me anything." When he was elected he did the electric slide dance to show that he was a regular guy. He also said "I could help a city, that I feel that I'm indebted to because the city I grew up in was nothing like the city I inherited. In the 1940s the city, started to go down hill, now it's starting to return."⁶

He advises future politicians to build a foundation of honesty and dedication. "You are here to serve the people and the job takes you away from your family. You can build coalitions, but you don't have to compromise your principles."⁷ As an interesting aside, to Thompson, politicians are always male and not female.

During his closing comments he said:

When I came, I was like an appointed man, a tool someone put here to be in control of nothing, nothing more than a puppet. But when you come, it's a job that takes hold of you, if you really care about it. I'm just an individual who just loves the city of Camden and wants to see it do better.⁸

As a side note, Mayor Thompson informed me that keeping appointments are very important to him. He kept his appointment with me in spite of the fact that he was notified that at the time, former First Lady Hillary Clinton called to meet with him at the last minute. Upon learning this, I thanked him again for the interview and left.

SUMMARY NOTE

Although Thompson tried to revive the city, he was (as anyone would have been) overwhelmed by the city's problems and lack of resources. The Democratic city machine dumped him in 1993 in favor of School Board President Arnold W. Webster. Webster's campaign slogan was "Hope, Change, and Responsibility." Webster wanted to continue the development of the Cooper Plaza Historic District, the Central Business District and the Waterfront Developments. But he struggled for power with the Hispanic community, the

Delaware River Port Authority and the County Government. Strong opposition by City Council President Milton Milan, along with Webster's indictment for misuse of School Board funds ended his career. It would seem that the words of Aaron Thompson about being open and honest came to haunt those who later became Mayor of Camden. Milton Milan became the first Hispanic mayor of Camden in 1998. 40% of the population was Hispanic, but Milan had to deal with feuding Puerto Rican groups even as Dominicans, Nicaraguans, and other Spanish-Speaking people arrived with their particular concerns and the need to be assimilated. The Dominicans alone had over 100 corner bodegas (grocery stores). There was an increase of Cambodians, Koreans and other Asian Americans, all in need of different and varying types of support. This diverse Hispanic group quickly became too difficult for Milan to govern or manage. In the end, he was indicted and convicted for corruption in 2000.[9]

According to rankings based on crime statistics, on November 22, 2004 Camden became the Nation's most dangerous city, inheriting the dubious title from Detroit, Michigan. The current mayor of Camden (Fall 2009), African American, The Honorable Gwendolyn A. Faison has her hands full.

Small towns have also been venues for electing African American mayors. Glenarden, Maryland is a case in point.

NOTES

1. Aaron Thompson, (1993). Personal interview, (recorded on audiotape by Deborah F. Atwater).
2. Aaron Thompson, Interview.
3. Aaron Thompson, Interview.
4. Aaron Thompson, Interview.
5. Aaron Thompson, Interview.
6. Aaron Thompson, Interview.
7. Aaron Thompson, Interview.
8. Aaron Thompson, Interview.
9. Jeffrey M. Dorwat (2001). *Camden County, New Jersey: The Making of a Metropolitan community, 1626-2000.* Camden, New Jersey: Rutgers University Press, 156-157.

Chapter Five

Marvin Wilson:
Mayor as Purveyor of Hope,
Glenarden, MD

Glenarden came into existence in 1910 when W.R. Smith purchased a group of properties 10 miles east of Washington, D.C. and established a community of 15 people. The charter, granted on March 30, 1939 made Glenarden the third predominately Black incorporated town in the state of Maryland. In 1906 Glenarden was mostly farmland and included the Palmer Plantation. Three decades later it was a predominantly black rural community. The Civic Association of this African American middle-class suburb petitioned the State Legislature for incorporation as the Town of Glenarden and W.H. Swann was elected its first Mayor. Under Swann's administration rapid changes were made; residents were now able to enjoy home heating with gas and electricity and improved road construction. Glenarden (current population approximately 10,000) was designed for Black GIs (Palmer Park for White GIs). With its quiet rural atmosphere and proximity to D.C., it has become the place for Blacks who wanted to live in the suburbs and its population has risen.[1]

In 1941 ex-Police Chief, James R. Cousins, Jr. became Glenardern's second Mayor and served until 1970. In 1943 Mayor Cousins, along with Councilman Robert Hawkins; W.B. Clark; William C. Johnson and William W. Smith decided a "Town Hall" was needed. Council Hawkins and his wife Sarah, owners of the proposed building site, volunteered to trade their property for another lot owned by the town. Mrs. Hawkins organized the women's Town Hall Club and raised $1,800 to fund the initial construction and it was completed at a cost of approximately $8,000.[2]

The town celebrated its 50th anniversary in 1989. In April of 1994, the Town Council adopted a resolution to change the name of the community to City of Glenarden. The City of Glenarden takes particular pride in its youth

programs. The Midnight Basketball League, Inc. targets school drop-outs and
the jobless, ages 17-21. During the summer months the league plays three
games per night, three nights a week between 10:00 pm and 2:00 am. The
National Midnight Basketball League was founded in 1986 by the late G. Van
Standifier in response to escalating crime rates and drug related activities in
the township. Initially the program was funded entirely by the local business
community and staffed by volunteers. The program proved to be a source of
pride even for those who opposed it at the outset. As a result of the program,
crime has been reduced by 60%. There are now at least 50 chapters Nation-
wide and in Puerto Rico with approximately 10,000 youths participating.
Before each event, youth attend a one hour workshop and discuss topics like
HIV/AIDS and drug and alcohol abuse prevention, and learn job interview
and financial management skills. There are usually 8-10 teams in a chapter
and 10-12 players per team and they are given sports equipment, shoes and
T-shirts.[3]

On April 12, 1991, Former President George H.W. Bush visited Glenarden
to celebrate National Community Points of Light Week. The President named
the Midnight Basketball League, Inc. the 124th Point of Light.

When Marvin Wilson arrived in Glenarden in 1964 he encountered prejudice. When I interviewed Mayor Wilson in June 1994, he had been in office
for three years and had served as an elected official for 23 years, serving on
the Council Board. He ran for Mayor so he could have more control over
the issues affecting the city, one of which was economic development with
Urban Renewal being the first phase. When $555,000 in municipal bonds
had been sold he decided to create new streets throughout the city at a cost
of $1.5 million. New street signs were to be uniform and large enough so
senior citizens could better read them. In his research, he visited Reston
and Columbia to get modern ideas for the signs. His main concern was
economic development and he wanted to build better houses, better play-
grounds, better parks and better commercial areas. He had promoted this
agenda as a Council member but it wasn't until he became Mayor that he
was able to go to the State and discover how he could move forward to accomplish it. For the Community Development Block program he purchased
2.2 acres from the FDIC, and an old bank which he hoped to develop as a
town center.[4]

Prior to his political career he was a professional cryptographer for the
National Security Agency at Fort Mead, retiring in 1991. Having a keen in-
terest in design, he majored in Commercial Art; using his talent, he designed
Glenarden's Town Seal in 1975. As Mayor, Wilson said, "I'm in a position to
try to sell my dreams and my ideas. In essence, it is hope for the future of the
town."[5]

MEDIA COVERAGE

I've been treated fairly by the papers, *Glenarden Express* and the *Journal* newspapers as well as the Black newspaper, *Prince George's Post.* The TV station-B10 good, bad, or indifferent. What you see is what you get. They broadcast some public meetings first Monday of every month. Some members of the council weren't thrilled with coverage especially when discussing personnel matters. More people watched than they thought. Some people thought that the differences and anger aired will cause trouble for the Mayor and the Council Board.[6]

Knowing that those residents knew him to be an honest person, Mayor Wilson felt that the coverage would not hurt him.

LEADERSHIP STYLE

The Council members who viewed him as a dictator he responded:

I'm a mover and a shaker and I don't like to wait to do things. As long as I know I'm doing right and as long as I'm abiding by the charter, I don't feel that I have to go to the legislative body to get permission to do a lot of things.[7]

He is convinced that his military background is a strong factor in his leadership style.

"Maybe I'm an independent person, I think that might come out of the fact that for 39 years I worked for an agency where being independent is a part of the job. Maybe, I'm not perfect, a lot of things want to be a part of it equally when they see it it's done."[8]

PUBLIC SPEAKING STYLE

I don't give myself credit, but other people do. I stick to detail, I try to be very clear. Once a professor told me, when you're speaking to a large audience, you scan your audience and you find a person that you feel would be less likely to understand what you're saying and you speak to him clear enough and if you reach him, you'll reach everyone in the room. Therefore, I look for an Average Joe. I try to use simple, clear words, and I try to be precise, give detail, and I can answer questions clear enough. You can judge by the number of questions that are asked.[9]

Mayor Wilson writes his own speeches and has someone check for grammatical errors and asks for feedback as to the speech's clarity.

BIG AND SMALL CITIES

Commenting on his visits to Chicago and Detroit he said:

> I'm not interested in going to the county or state. The change from town to city was a symbol for growth close to the people, driving to work. Some things may work for big cities, like they work here, i.e. the Midnight Basketball Program. There is a mix of section 8 housing with regular housing in Glenarden and this was done by design to provide incentive. Seniors are on Main Street. We want them to see traffic and kids, see life. We have services for them, lawn care, cable TV, and trash removal. Section 8-Hawkins Manor can look like Know Hill, Colmer Manor.[10]

Mayor Wilson concludes: "It's nobody's business what you pay for rent and there's no reason why this couldn't work in big cities instead of the 32 story buildings that are reservations."[11]

In our discussion of his April 1994 meeting with President Clinton at the National Black Mayors Conference, Mayor Wilson said that as Governor, former President Clinton knew about small towns and cities and that he believed President Clinton was supportive of Black mayors. He and the former President discussed money and grants like the Casey foundation. Former President Clinton was also aware of the Midnight Basketball Program.

NEED FOR COALITIONS

Mayor Wilson:

> I appeal to liberals, conservatives, businessmen, professional, blue collar. I went to every door and my message is clear to everyone even to drug dealers. All people respect me. I also know that people in high income areas have different needs from people in low income areas.[12]

When I asked Mayor Wilson how he wanted his term in office to be remembered, he responded:

> I want people to know that I stressed economic development. I wanted people to live better and have better services, better schools. Why not use bricks instead of cinder blocks. Why not change the design and color to make people feel human. I want people to say, 'He made a difference, he made me want to help other people do better.'[13]

I concluded the interview with a question regarding the future of Black Mayors. In general, Mayor Wilson views small towns and cities as venues in which Black mayors can make a visible difference in the quality of life for people in general and Black people in particular, saying simply, "We need design and beauty in our neighborhoods."[14] These words indicate Mayor Wilson's vision and hope for the future of small cities and Black mayors.

Even though some cities have elected Black mayors in the past, there are a few cities that have given a young African American male or female an opportunity to lead. Detroit, Michigan gave such an opportunity to one young man.

NOTES

1. The Town of Glenarden's 50th Anniversary Celebration Booklet, Town of Glenarden, 8600 Glenarden Parkway, Glenarden, MD 20706. (1989) 38-39.
2. The Town of Glenarden's 50th Anniversary Celebration Booklet, Town of Glenarden, 39.
3. Marvin Wilson (1994). Personal interview. (Recorded on audiotape by Deborah F. Atwater). 3 June.
4. Marvin Wilson, Interview.
5. Marvin Wilson, Interview.
6. Marvin Wilson, Interview.
7. Marvin Wilson, Interview.
8. Marvin Wilson, Interview.
9. Marvin Wilson, Interview.
10. Marvin Wilson, Interview.
11. Marvin Wilson, Interview.
12. Marvin Wilson, Interview.
13. Marvin Wilson, Interview.
14. Marvin Wilson, Interview.

Chapter Six

Kwame Malik Kilpatrick: Mayor as Rising Star/Fallen Angel, Detroit, MI

HISTORY OF DETROIT

During the Prohibition Era a thriving underground business developed as mobsters shipped liquor across the Great Lakes of Canada. Initially, the Great Depression of the 1930s hit Detroit hard, but the automobile industry managed to survive. The modern movement for labor unions began with a famous battle between union organizers and police at the Ford River Rouge plant in 1937. Led by Walter Reuther, the United Auto Workers survived and grew stronger during sit-down strikes and organizing drives.[1]

POST-WAR ECONOMIC BOOM

Major shifts occurred in Detroit's demographics after World War II. The post-war economic boom was accompanied by the construction of a network of freeways that decimated Detroit's old neighborhoods while making possible the exponential growth of suburbs. For a while, downtown Detroit remained the thriving center of the metropolitan area, its population peaking at 2.1 million in the late 1950s. In the 1960s it became a cultural center for the nation, exporting the most popular music of the era, the catchy rhythm-and-blues known as the Motown sound.[2]

But as more prosperous people fled the city and left poorer ones behind, racial tensions heightened. They exploded in the infamous 1967 riots which left dozens dead and further hastened White flight. The city plunged into a long decline, as key components of business, industry and culture shifted to the suburbs.

Civic leaders made efforts to turn things around, beginning with the building of the Renaissance Center office-hotel-retail complex in 1973. For years, the Renaissance Center remained an isolated fortress with little effect on surrounding areas. The city continued to lose people and money, and its fine housing suffered from neglect and abandonment. The automobile industry was hit hard by a severe recession caused by rising oil prices and competition from Japanese imports. Factories in the city closed and thousands of good-paying jobs for unskilled workers disappeared never to return.[3]

DOWNTOWN'S RESURGENCE

In the 1980s, Joe Louis Arena was constructed as the home of the Detroit Red Wings and the Millender Center opened near the Renaissance Center. Red Wings owner Mike Ilitch saved the Fox Theater and its revival began a genuine downtown resurgence in the 1990s. Through that decade, Detroiters debated the merits of casinos and a new baseball stadium, finally approving both ideas. During the 1990s the city's population finally stabilized at around a million people and business investment began returning to the city.[4] But the current recession has hit Detroit harder than most other cities as evidenced its unemployment rate of 22% and the need for the Big Three auto companies to seek billions of dollars in Federal funds for support.

The growth of the suburbs has permanently changed the city's landscape. Most jobs, hotels, restaurants, shopping centers and entertainment facilities are now outside the city limits, creating a sprawling metropolitan area that remains heavily dependent on the automobile. Yet a more unified approach to the area's problems has civic leaders optimistic. Detroit retains its rich cultural treasures, its vibrant entertainment and dining scene, and above all its strength as a genuine melting pot, with immigrants from around the world bringing their own cuisine, traditions and religions. It has proven to be a re-silient place and one of America's greatest cities.[5]

Unlike some of the other mayors covered in this book, embattled former Mayor Kwame Kilpatrick of Detroit was not the first Black mayor of the city. In fact, the city's first Black mayor was Coleman Young, elected in 1973, a position he held until 1993. Mayor Coleman died on November 12, 1997 and the city elected another Black mayor, Dennis Archer who served until 2001.

KILPATRICK'S BACKGROUND

Kwame Malik Kilpatrick, the youngest person ever to be elected mayor of Detroit was born in Detroit in Michigan on June 6, 1970, the son of US Rep-resentative Carolyn Cheeks Kilpatrick and Bernard Kilpatrick. Taking office in January 2002, he was sometimes referred to as "America's First Hip-Hop Mayor", in part, because he wore an earring in his left ear. He subsequently removed the earring during the 2005 campaign and has since not replaced it.

At 6'4" and at one time weighing nearly 300 pounds, he presents a commanding presence, thus it is not surprising to learn that he was the captain of the football team during his college days as Florida A&M.

Kilpatrick, reared on the city's West side, argued that he had politics in his blood because of his family role models. His mother, Congresswoman Carolyn Cheeks Kilpatrick served 18-years as State Representative for Detroit's 9th District. His father, Bernard Kilpatrick worked for the Wayne County Executive.

Kwame attended Cass Technical High School and attended Florida A&M University, graduating with honors. He is a member of Alpha Phi Alpha Fraternity, the oldest intercollegiate Greek-letter fraternity established for African Americans. He earned a law degree from the Detroit College of Law (now a part of Michigan State University). Kilpatrick received his Bachelor of Science degree in political science in 1992. He began his teaching career at Rickards High School, but it wasn't long before he returned to Detroit to accept a teaching position at Marcus Garvey Academy and took on additional roles of basketball coach and mentor. However, when the opportunity arose to enter politics he seized the opportunity.

Congresswoman Cheeks Kilpatrick decided to transition from state representative to U.S. Congresswoman in 1995. She won the position of U.S. Representative leaving her seat available to her son who won her seat in 1996. Kilpatrick married Carlita Poles whom he met at FAMU and they became the parents of twin sons, Jalil and Jelani.

Kilpatrick maintained a residence in Detroit and divided his time between Lansing and his home in Detroit. By 1998 he had helped to develop the $675 million dollar Clean Michigan Initiative and was able to designate 60 per cent of the funds to Detroit as it is the state's largest city and the one most in need. He also raised millions to fight lead poisoning in the city because there were more child-related lead poisoning cases reported in Detroit than in the rest of the state combined.

He was busy doing great things for the city when the opportunity to run for State House Minority Leader opened in 2000. Although many thought he was too young for the position, he ran and was elected in January, 2001. He set numerous precedents. Not only was he the first African-American chosen for this position, at age 30 was the youngest person ever to hold the position. His star was on the rise.

In April of 2001 Dennis Archer announced that he would not be running for re-election. With this announcement Kilpatrick saw an opportunity to take the job that he had been thinking and dreaming about since 1980. Again, people thought that he was too young to lead a city infamous for its decades of decay. The BBC reflected the thoughts of many Detroit voters when they commented that his presence was commanding and his call for government reform much welcomed.[6]

Kilpatrick joined the race, trailing in a group of 21 candidates. But when the people voted in the primary election on September 11, 2001, he walked away with 50.2 percent of the votes (his closet front runner Detroit Councilman Gil Hill received 34.4 percent). Gil Hill was a former Detroit police detective who had also appeared in the *Beverly Hills Cop* films. Kilpatrick won the election for the office on November 6, 2001 and was sworn in January 4, 2002 as mayor of Detroit. In his inaugural speech, he outlined his three point initiative for the term:

1. Improve the police department
2. Begin Mayor's Time, a program for the city's youth and
3. Head a citywide clean-up effort.

This time marked another personal change for him; his wife, Carlita, had just given birth to his third son, Jonas. She wanted to work in partnership with him; to stand by his side and help him realize his dreams of civic service. Kilpatrick's dream was to let the people of Detroit know how sincere he was about creating a better city. "My entire family dwells within the walls of the city of Detroit," he said to the *Detroit News*, "This position is personal to me. It's much more than just politics."[7]

Kilpatrick was a member of the Mayors Against Illegal Guns Coalition, an organization formed in 2006 co-chaired by New York City Mayor Michael Bloomberg and Boston Mayor Thomas Menino. In 2004, Kilpatrick even briefly addressed the 2004 Democratic National Convention. He was gaining national prominence.

HIS EXIT: A SLOW DESCENT

By April 2005 Kilpatrick's approval rating in Detroit was sharply declining due to the scandals and a perceived lack of improvements in the city. As a result, the April 17, 2005 *Time Magazine* listed him as one of the three worst big-city mayors in the United States, sharing that dubious title with Dick Murphy of San Diego and John F. Street of Philadelphia.

The Detroit Free Press in May, 2005 reported that over the first 33 months of his term, Kilpatrick had charged over $210,000 on his city-issued credit card for travel, meals and entertainment. In October 2005 Kilpatrick caused controversy with an advertisement which compared media criticism of him to lynch mobs.

2005 RE-ELECTION CAMPAIGN

In 2005, both Kilpatrick and his challenger Freman Hendrix, both Democrats, initially claimed victory. But when the final votes were tallied it was clear that he had won a second term in office. In the months that preceded the election, when he became the first Detroit incumbent mayor to come in second in a primary, several reporters from the mainstream media declared that his political career was over. Pre-election polls had predicted that Hendrix was certain to win. But surprisingly, Kilpatrick won with 53 percent of the vote and he was all too eager to point out his accomplishments in the effort to revitalize Detroit which included improved city services, construction of new homes and downtown.

In July of 2006, Kilpatrick was hospitalized in Houston, Texas with diverticulitis. His personal physician, Dr. Aaron Maddox indicated that Kilpatrick's condition might have been caused by his high-protein weight-loss diet. That same July, Detroit's City Council voted unanimously to approve Kilpatrick's tax plan in hope of some relief for the city's high property tax rates. The mainstream media kept Kilpatrick under close scrutiny and on May 8, 2007, WXYZ-TV reported that Kilpatrick used $8,600 from his secret Kilpatrick Civic Fund to take his wife, three sons and babysitter on a week-long vacation to the five-star California resort, the La Costa Resort and Spa. The fund, controlled by Kilpatrick's sister and friends, was created to improve the city of Detroit through voter education, economic empowerment and crime prevention. Accounting and tax experts said his use of the fund was a violation of IRS regulations.

Several months later Kilpatrick's troubles continued when in August 2007 he was sued by two ex-members of his bodyguard staff for violation of the Whistleblower Law. The men claimed that Kilpatrick fired them in retaliation for their investigation into his personal actions. The trial ended on September 11, 2007 when after three hours of deliberation, the jury awarded the plaintiffs $6.5 million in damages. Within minutes of the verdict, many accused Kilpatrick of delivering an angry speech in front of City Hall in which he blamed the "wrong verdict" on white suburban jurors. A separate article attributes the following quote to Kilpatrick, "There's race in this and we run from it in this region. And I think it's impossible for us to move forward as a region without confronting this head-on. But I don't want what has happened in the past 24 months to be erased by what has happened in the last two days."[8] In a September 12 *Detroit Free Press* article, one of the jurors taking offense at Kilpatrick words said that Kilpatrick was a "spoiled little brat who has been caught with his hand in the cookie jar, was sent to the corner and is now pouting."[9] When Kilpatrick's mother, Congresswoman Carolyn Cheeks Kilpatrick appeared on Detroit Station WXYZ, she said the jury was wrong and that the City would appeal the verdict.

MANOOGIAN MANSION PARTY

Kilpatrick's controversies began at a wild party alleged to have occurred in the fall of 2002, involving strippers at the official residence of the mayor— the city-owned Manoogian Mansion. Former members of the mayor's Executive Protection Unit claimed that the mayor's wife, Carlita Kilpatrick came home unexpectedly and upon discovering Kwame with the strippers began to attack one of the women. Allegations began to surface after Officer Harold C. Nelthrope contacted the Internal Affairs unit of the Detroit Police in April 2003 to have them investigate abuses by the mayor's Executive Protection Unit (EPU). Mayor Kilpatrick denied all allegations and rumors of misconduct by him or his security team. An investigation by Michigan Attorney General Mike Cox and the Michigan State Police found no evidence of said party. Nelthrope and Gary A. Brown, head of the Detroit Police Department's Internal Affairs Division alleged that they were fired by the administration in retaliation for investigating the Mayor and other superiors. Nelthrope and Brown filed a whistleblower lawsuit and were awarded an $8.4 million settlement.[10]

Two other officers in the Detroit Police Department, Walt Harris and Alvin Bowman, correctly claimed they were retaliated against for their involvement in investigations that highlighted the mayor's misconduct. Harris, a former member of the EPU was identified by the administration as cooperating with the State's investigation of the mayor and subsequently suffered a smear campaign in the media by the Kilpatrick administration.

THE MURDER OF TAMARA GREENE

Tamara Greene was a 27-year-old exotic dancer who went by the name "Strawberry." Ms. Greene was allegedly attacked by the mayor's wife, Carlita on the same night she allegedly performed at the Manoogian Mansion party. While sitting in her car with her boyfriend, Greene was shot multiple times with a .40 caliber Glock handgun. Although the official statement by Detroit Police Department claims that Ms. Greene was shot three times, sources from Homicide Division of DPD later claimed that she was shot 18 times. Her boyfriend was wounded but was not fired upon after the white Chevrolet Trail Blazer driven by the shooter(s) turned around and drove by a second time. This fact led Bowman to conclude that Greene was the intended target rather than her 32-year-old boyfriend.

Ms. Greene was murdered on April 30, 2003 near the intersection of Roselawn and West Outer Drive at around 3:40 am. An earlier failed attempt on her life strengthened the theory that this was a "deliberate hit" by a member of the Detroit Police Department, a theory that Bowman would investigate. He alleges this investigation was the reason he was taken off of the case and transferred out of the Homicide Division. Based on their belief her murder was a deliberate attack to keep her from talking to the investigating officers who investigated the rumors that she attended the party at the mayoral Manoogian Mansion, Greene's family filed a Federal lawsuit against the city of Detroit for $150 million. In an attempt to ascertain if city officials blocked the investigation into Greene's murder, access to the text message transmissions of Kilpatrick, police chief Ella Bully-Cummings and dozens of other city employees was granted when a judge ruled in favor of Norman Yatooma, the attorney representing Greene's 14-year-old son. Yatooma also asked for text messages exchanged by all city employees and their GPS positions occurring between 1:30 a.m. and 5:30 a.m. on the night of the murder.[11]

City Attorneys paid a retainer of $24,950 for attorneys to represent the city. City policy mandates that contracts of $25,000 or more be approved by the City Council. Councilwoman Sheila Cockrel asserts that the amount paid "is small for a retainer" and "I think this is probably somebody's effort to get a deposit to a lawyer on an expedited basis in a case that's got a lot of scrutiny."[12] This was at least the second time the Kilpatrick administration avoided Council approval by entering into contracts just below the $25,000 threshold. A Lincoln Navigator SUV leased for the Kilpatrick family in 2005 used city funds in the amount of $24,995.[13]

In a sworn affidavit, Joyce Carolyn Rogers, a former employee for the Detroit Police Department, stated that she read a police report in the fall of 2002 which involved the mayor's wife, Carlita Kilpatrick, assaulting Greene during the alleged Manoogian Mansion party. Rogers stated that the affidavit that Mrs. Kilpatrick witnessed Greene touching the mayor "in a manner that upset the mayor's wife," and that Mrs. Kilpatrick left the room and returned with a wooden object and began assaulting Greene; two other men then stepped in to restrain the mayor's wife.[14]

THE INDICTMENT

A rising star in the Democratic Party, Mayor Kwame Kilpatrick was indicted on March 24, 2008 for perjury.

The *Associated Press* reported:

> Mayor Kwame Kilpatrick, a one-time rising star and Detroit's youngest elected leader, was charged Monday with perjury and other counts after sexually explicit text messages contradicted his sworn denials of an affair with a top aide.
>
> Wayne County Prosecutor Kym Worthy also charged the popular yet polarizing 37-year-old mayor with obstruction of justice and misconduct in office.
>
> Former Chief of Staff Christine Beatty, 37, who also denied under oath that she and Kilpatrick had a romantic relationship in 2002 and 2003, was charged with perjury and obstruction of justice.
>
> "Some have suggested that the issues in this case are personal or private," Worthy said.
>
> "The justice system has been severely mocked and the public trust trampled on. . . . This case is about as far from being a private matter as one can get," she said.[15]

The text messages published by the *Free Press* revealed a romantic discourse. . .

> "I'm madly in love with you," Kilpatrick wrote on Oct. 3, 2002.
>
> "I hope you feel that way for a long time," Beatty replied. "In case you haven't noticed, I am madly in love with you, too!"
>
> In all, Kilpatrick faces charges of conspiracy to obstruct justice, obstruction of justice, misconduct in office, perjury in a court proceeding and two counts of perjury other than in a court proceeding.[16]

THE FUTURE FOR THE CITY AND MAYOR KILPATRICK

After an extraordinary day that saw him plead guilty to two felonies, Detroit Mayor Kwame Kilpatrick spoke for the first time publicly on the evening of September 4, 2008 in a televised speech that was part-apology, part campaign speech, "I've always said that you need to stand strong for the City of Detroit...but sometimes standing strong means stepping down."

With his mother U.S. Rep. Carolyn Cheeks Kilpatrick watching, Kilpatrick said, "I want to emphasize tonight that I take full responsibility for my actions . . . our challenge now is to put the anguish and the turmoil of recent months behind us."

Kilpatrick then proceeded to take light jabs at Gov. Jennifer Granholm, who he said put her efforts toward his removal above the many other problems facing the state, but added that he would continue to support her.

"I'm stepping down because the new spirit of this city, the new expectations and standards that we've set for excellence in the past six and a half years has been tangled up in what I believe is the pursuit of many people's own political ambitions, even our governor, Jennifer Granholm, who I wish well."

"Rather than focusing on the huge issues that are facing our state, from the record home foreclosures, the lack of affordable health- care, a record unemployment in our state, Kwame Kilpatrick was at the top of her list," he said. "I wish her well and hope that the same tenacity, the same professionalism, if you will, and intensity that went around putting together a quasi-administrative court will also be the same tenacity to solve the problems of the people of the state of Michigan."[17]

Granholm's spokeswoman Liz Boyd responded: "The Governor wishes Godspeed to the mayor and his family. With this behind us, leaders of our State and Detroit can devote 100 percent of their attention to growing the economy and creating jobs." Kilpatrick also said he would support City Council President Kenneth Cockrel Jr. when he became mayor, but warned that running Detroit was a lot different than leading the City Council.

Before launching into a litany of his accomplishments as mayor, Kilpatrick said, "To those who have supported me throughout the years....I thank you with all my heart ...I know that supporting me has not always been easy, but it has not been boring either."

He said that Cockrel inherits a city "in much better shape than the city I inherited seven years ago. Under this administration, Detroit has become an example of progress and resilience. I am proud of the fact that we as a community have been able to accomplish so much..."[18]

He praised his wife, Carlita saying that she was "the strongest woman that I've met in my entire life, the person with the most beautiful spirit, she can be a soldier at one minute and absolutely endearing the next, someone who took a wretch like me and said I am standing by you through thick and through thin..." "This city always gets up. I want to tell you, Detroit, that you done set me up for a comeback."[19]

THE PLEA DEAL THAT ENDED KILPATRICK'S TENURE

Kilpatrick's guilty plea ended an eight-month drama that had transfixed the region, paralyzed much of city business and halted a political career that once held great promise.

Kilpatrick plead guilty to two felony counts of obstructing justice by committing perjury. He would spend four months in jail, pay up to $1 million dollars in restitution, and serve five years' probation. He also agreed not to run for office during that five-year span.

In addition, the mayor agreed to a no-contest plea to one count of felonious assault for shoving a sheriff's deputy who had tried to serve a subpoena on one of Kilpatrick's friends. He agreed to serve four months on that charge, but it was to be served concurrently with the other sentence.

The deal also called for Kilpatrick to turn over his State pension to the City of Detroit (which would be applied to the $8.4 million to settle two whistle-blower lawsuits three former police officers filed against the city. The mayor was charged with eight felony counts including conspiracy; perjury; misconduct in office, and obstruction of justice when the *Free Press* revealed in January that the mayor lied on the witness stand during a police whistle-blower trial and gave misleading testimony about whether he intended to fire a deputy police chief investigating allegations of wrongdoing by members of his inner circle.

In a rushed monotone, before a standing-room only audience, Kilpatrick told Wayne Circuit Judge David Groner: "I lied under oath in the case of Gary Brown and Harold Nelthrope versus the city of Detroit ... I did so with the intent to mislead the court and jury, to impede and obstruct the disposition of justice."[20]

Moments after Groner praised the lawyers for their work reaching a deal, Kilpatrick summoned his wife, kissed her and went back into a side room.

"Justice has finally been served," University of Detroit Mercy law professor Larry Dubin said that morning. "The deal that the Mayor agreed to . . . is a major victory for the prosecutor, the mayor and the people of the City of Detroit and State of Michigan."[21]

Dubin, who has been outspoken in his criticism of the mayor, praised Wayne County Prosecutor Kym Worthy.

"For the way she prosecuted this case. She has demonstrated integrity in holding a public official accountable for serious criminal violations that constituted serious breaches of the public trust," Dubin said.[22]

Kilpatrick's mother, Michigan Rep. Carolyn Cheeks Kilpatrick issued a statement that same afternoon. "While my heart is heavy, I support Mayor Kilpatrick's decision to do what he believes is best for his family, our family, and the citizens of Detroit," she said. "I would like to thank all those who have encouraged the Mayor and our family with your prayers, cards, and other expressions of support. I ask that you continue to pray for the Mayor and his family and the city of Detroit during this difficult time."[23]

He shook hands with Christine Beatty, his former chief of staff and ex-lover. Beatty's lawyers had Groner delay her separate criminal case for a week while she tried to hammer out her own plea deal.

Stern-faced throughout the proceedings, First Lady Carlita Kilpatrick sat in the audience a few feet behind her husband. It was the first time she had been in a courtroom with Beatty since the scandal started in January.

Kilpatrick's lawyers and Wayne County Assistant Prosecutor Robert Moran began the day at the Cadillac Place State Office Building, where they met with Gov. Jennifer Granholm for approximately 45 minutes. When they updated the Governor on the plea agreement she canceled the historic removal proceedings that had begun the day before which most likely would have resulted in Kilpatrick's removal from office.

In January, the *Free Press* published text messages exchanged between Kilpatrick and Beatty on city-issued pagers, proving they had perjured themselves when they testified under oath in a police whistle-blower trial the previous year that they were not having nor did they have an intimate relationship. They also had given misleading testimony about the firing of a top police official, Gary Brown. Nelthrope was another police officer who sued with Brown, both alleging their careers were ruined because of their involvement in an internal affairs investigation that could have led to the discovery of extramarital philandering by Kilpatrick.

Worthy cited the *Free Press* investigation in March, when she charged Kilpatrick with eight felonies and Beatty with seven. The charges included perjury, conspiracy, obstruction of justice and misconduct in office.

Mayor Kilpatrick was released from jail on February 3, 2009 after Kilpatrick completed 99 days of his four month sentence in the Detroit County Jail. He was greeted by two dozen reporters and a handful of onlookers. His defense attorney, Willie E. Gary said that Kilpatrick would be heading to Texas for a job interview and Kilpatrick was about to accept a position in Texas with Convisint, an affiliate of Detroit-based Compuware Corporation (*Free Press*). Kilpatrick reunited with his wife and children in Texas and said that his jail time was "an incredibly purifying process."[24] Several attempts to contact Mayor Kilpatrick for an interview by me yielded no response.

And so goes the story of Kwame Kilpatrick's meteoric rise and his untimely fall from grace. Former Mayor Kilpatrick had the usual general issues that he apparently could manage, but it was his situationally unique issues and scandals that eventually brought his downfall or his fall from grace. Yet as his speech indicated, Mr. Kilpatrick believes that he will live to see a better day. As an aside, the voters of Detroit, decided to elect another African American mayor, former basketball star and business man Dave Bing.

NOTES

1. http://www.schmap.com/detroit/introduction_history/.

2. http://www.schmap.com/detroit/introduction_history/.

3. http://www.schmap.com/detroit/introduction_history/.

4. http://www.schmap.com/detroit/introduction_history/.

5. Copyright 1999-2005 Wcities, Inc. All Rights Reserved. Contact Wcities.

6. BBC Report.

7. http://www.answers.com/topic/kwame-kilpatrick-p.3.

8. Stephen Henderson, *Detroit News*, September 13, 2007.

9. http://www.answers.com/topic/kwame-kilpatrick.

10. http://www.answers.com/topic/kwame-kilpatrick.

11. http://www.answers.com/topic/kwame-kilpatrick.

12. http://www.answers.com/topic/kwame-kilpatrick.

13. http://www.answers.com/topic/kwame-kilpatrick.

14. http://www.answers.com/topic/kwame-kilpatrick.

15. AP Report, March 28, 2008, Name That Party: Detroit Mayor Kwame Kilpatrick Indicted.

16. Kilpatrick to city: 'There's another day for me'116 "Fallen, yet resolute, mayor says he accepts responsibility for actions" by M.L. Elrick, Jim Schaefer, Joe Swickard and Ben Schmitt, *Free Press* Staff Writers, September 4, 2008.

17. Schafer, et. al, "There's another day for me."

18. Schafer, et. al, "There's another day for me."

19. Schafer, et. al, "There's another day for me."

20. AP Report, March 28, 2008.

21. AP Report, March 28, 2008.

22. AP Report, March 28, 2008.

23. Schafer, et. al, "There's another day for me."

24. Marti Parham and AP reporters, "Detroit's Ex-Mayor Finishes Jail Term, Seeks New Job," *Jet*, 24.

Chapter Seven

Conclusion

I have briefly examined the administrations of six African American Mayors: Mayor as Technocrat and Pioneer, Wilson Goode, Philadelphia; Mayor as Educator, James H. Sills, Jr. Wilmington, Delaware; Woman Reformer, Sharon Pratt Dixon Kelly, Washington, D.C.; Mayor as Caretaker, Aaron Thompson, Camden, New Jersey; Mayor as Purveyor of Hope, Marvin Wilson, Glenarden, Maryland; and Mayor as Rising Star and Fallen Angel, Kwame Kilpatrick, Detroit, Michigan.

Some were mayors of large cities others of small towns, yet they all shared a sincere love for their cities and a deep and sincere desire to serve the public; not only African Americans, but all the citizens. Each one came to office at the lowest, most perilous point in their city's history. Forces such as deindustrialization, White flight and residential segregation set the stage for the victories of Black mayors and exacerbated the obstacles they confronted. Each one had innovative and unique ways of dealing with those numerous and complex problems. It is also amazing that some mayors, long after their term in office has ended continue to have a real concern for the future of their cities and citizens.

In regard to their public speaking abilities; most of them considered themselves to be direct and that they could relate well to a diverse audience. Most believed they received fair press coverage from mainstream and Black-owned media. However, all of them felt that they were held to higher standards and had insufficient time to turn things around in their cities.

In review; Black Mayoral Candidates and Mayors face the following challenges:

1. Perceived to be special-interest candidates for Blacks only and/or minorities.

2. If more than one African American enters the race, the issue of one of the candidates dropping out to preserve unity is placed and remains in the forefront of the campaign.
3. Must always demonstrate the ability to help all citizens sometimes to the detriment of Blacks.
4. The cities they inherit are usually in decay after years of neglect, but immediate turn-around of economy is expected. The miracle-worker, superman image is prevalent.
5. The competence and credibility question is always a factor.
6. Class issues for Black candidates may become intrusive.
7. Coalitions are more difficult to hold together when trying to expand the base.
8. Media coverage is vastly different for African Americans (Black press is still important and necessary).
9. Race is always an issue and sometimes gender.
10. Black voter education does not always translate into an organized, sustaining structure for future election of black officials.

WHERE DO WE GO FROM HERE?

The future of Black Mayors is at once both challenging and promising. But the mayoralties must be considered in the context of the changing demographics of the 21st Century. It is likely that all mayors would agree that building coalitions is a top and important priority.

In *The Presumed Alliance: The unspoken conflict between Latinos and Blacks and what it means for America*, Nicolas C. Vaca makes some relevant and pertinent arguments about current coalitions.

> In this united ideological march for enfranchisement, Blacks took the lead and the rest of the minorities supported them. The civil rights agenda was set by African Americans and the rest acquiesced. From the beginning African Americans outnumbered all other minorities and their numbers granted them an additional reason for assuming the leadership role. Without their numbers, any minority coalition would be weakened, and consequently not taken seriously. However, things have changed due to increased immigration both legal and illegal and exploding birthrates have swelled the ranks of both Asian Americans and Latinos.[1]

He goes on to say that,

> For a brief period, during the Black and Chicano social movements of the 1960s and 1970s, Blacks and Latinos worked on common issues and goals—some meaningful, some symbolic.[2]

An interesting example of this occurred in Houston.

> As the mayor's office in Houston is not merely a symbolic position, but one with significant power and control, it was significant that in 1997 that African American Lee P. Brown former Houston police chief was elected mayor by a 53% to 47% margin, defeating Republican businessman Rob Mosbacher with 26% of the White vote, 95% of the Black vote, and the Latino voters chose to split between Brown and Mosbacher.[3]

In 1989 a Black-Latino coalition was instrumental in electing New York Mayor, African American David Dinkins.

I agree with Vaca when he says:

> Tomorrow's America will be an America greatly influenced by Latinos and their culture, but it will also be one based on the history of Latinos in the United States, in which Latinos can be described as an ethnic patina set atop America's existing social, political, economic, and legal structures.[4]

Chris Thompson of the *Express-Times*, Easton, PA offers compelling insights on black political leaders (Dec.12, 2005). "The case of Ron Dellums in Oakland, California epitomizes an historic change in American politics. Dellums himself was always more than a machine politician; in fact, Rep. Barbara Lee called him "the father of coalition politics."[5]

But today, particularly in the West, an era of Black political power centered in urban enclaves is coming to an end. Latino migration is supplanting traditional African-American majorities into cities like Compton and Los Angeles, and a rising Black middle class is moving into the suburbs. California's inner cities are becoming less Black and the political machines that have run them for decades are gasping their last breath. No Black state legislator holds office north of Los Angeles County. Black politics is maturing beyond the language of grievance and adopting an increasingly middle-class, entrepreneurial character. Having outgrown identity politics, they are forcing Black leaders to run on their own merits in racially diverse districts. The election of New York's Republican Mayor, Michael Bloomberg, who received half of the Black vote and 30% of the Latino vote despite challenger Fernando Ferrer's deliberate campaign as a Latino candidate, attests to this change. There exists a demand for representative diversity and better government. Based on the increase in Latino numbers, (an increase of 50%, Blacks 36% in 2000), California Representative Maxine Waters may someday be challenged by a new generation of Latinos for her congressional seat.

There is a sense among all voters that competence matters as much if not more than ethnic representation. Thus, in the future we will see new and interesting coalitions forming around issues and their solutions. Representative

Barbara Lee of California states it best, "Coalition politics is about expanding opportunity, fostering prosperity, and valuing diversity. And that is a message that the majority of Americans believe in."[6]

African American mayors will continue to be a force in local politics as long as they continue to form coalitions and present a clear, appealing and inclusive message to all people. There may come a time in the twenty-first century when an African American male or female will be elected mayor to a city that is not in structural decay and/or financial ruin. African American mayors have the potential to unleash the creative energies of all people in how they live and thrive in cities. How they deal with general and situationally unique issues will continue to force African American mayors to be creative, innovative and daring. How they address the public and are perceived in the press will continue to have an impact on their success in governing cities. What better way to document their successes and or failures than in their own words.

NOTES

1. Nicolas C. Vaca, (2004). *The Presumed Alliance: The Unspoken Conflict Between Latinos and Blacks and What it Means for America*. New York, New York, Harper Collins, x, xi.

2. Vaca, *The Presumed Alliance*, 150.

3. Vaca, *The Presumed Alliance*, 152-153.

4. Vaca, *The Presumed Alliance*, 202.

5. Chris Thompson, (December 12, 2005). Rise of New Black Leaders. *The Express Times. Easton, PA*.

6. Chris Thompson, (December 12, 2005). Rise of New Black Leaders.

Bibliography

"A Pick With a Shovel: Promising to clean house, an anti-Barry reformer wins in D.C." *Time*, 24 September 1990:52.

Assefa, Hizkias and Paul Wahrhaftig. (1988). *Extremist Groups and Conflict Resolution: The MOVE Crisis in Philadelphia.* New York: Praeger Publishers.

Barrish, Cris. (1993). Delaware News Journal. Personal interview. (recorded on audio tape by Deborah F. Atwater) 27 October.

Bauman, John F. (1992). W. Wilson Goode: The Black mayor as urban entrepreneur. *Journal of Negro History.* Vol; 77. mp.3 (summer) 142-158."

Berardi, Gayle K., & Thomas W. Segady. "The Development of African American Newspapers in the American West: A Sociohistorical Perspective." *Journal of Negro History* 75 (Summer/Fall 1990): 96-111.

Bell, Janet Cheatham. (1986). *Famous Black Quotes* Chicago, Illinois, Sabavt Publications.

Bennet, James. "Bloat People," *The Washington Monthly*, September 1991, 27-36.

Biles, Roger. (Summer 1992). Black Mayors: A historical assessment. *Journal of Negro History.* Vol.77. no.3: 109-125.

Bitzer, Lloyd F. (1968). The rhetorical situation. *Philosophy and Rhetoric.* 1-15.

Black Enterprise. February 1982.

Black Entertainment Television: Personal Diary: Sharon Pratt Kelly, August 1, 1993. 10:30 AM.

Black Mayors Conference. (May 2003). www.blackmayors.org/members.html

Borger, Gloria. "Sharon Pratt Dixon: Like Other City Leaders, D.C.'s New Boss Needs A Miracle" *U.S. News and World Report*, 31 Dec. 1990, 72-73.

Business Week, 1970.

Colburn, David R. and Jeffrey S. Adler (Eds.). (2001). *African-American Mayors: Race, Politics, and the American city.* Urbana and Chicago: University of Illinois Press.

Cooke, Russell. (1993). Personal interview. (recorded on audio tape by Deborah F. Atwater) 1 October.

Cooke, Russell. (1992). *Philadelphia Inquirer*, C4.

District of Columbia available at: http://earthops.org/dcstatehood.html.

District of Columbia: *National Journal's The Almanac of American Politics 1996*, which was published in July of 1995,)

Dorwart, Jeffery M. (2001*). Camden County, New Jersey: The Making of a Metropolitan community, 1626-2000*. Camden, New Jersey: Rutgers University Press.

French, Mary Ann. "Who Is Sharon Pratt Dixon?," *Essence* (Apr. 1991).

Fulwood, III, Sam. "Mayor Sharon Pratt Dixon: Washington's New Hope. *Emerge*: February 1991, 36-38, 40.

Goode, Wilson W. (with Joann Stevens). (1992). In Goode Faith. Valley Forge, PA: Judson Press.

Goode, Wilson W. (1993). Personal interview. (recorded on audio tape by Deborah F. Atwater). 25 September.

http://www.blackpast.org/?q=aah/kelly-sharon-pratt-dixon-1944.

Hunter, Deborah Atwater F. (1978). The Aftermath of Carl Stokes: An analysis of political drama in the 1971 Cleveland mayoral campaign. *Journal of Black Studies* vol.8, no.3. March: 337-354.

Kaniss, Phyllis. (1995). *The Media and the Mayor's race: The Failure of Urban Political Reporting*. Bloomington, Indiana: Indiana University Press.

Kelly, Sharon Pratt Dixon. (1994). Speech at Howard University. (recorded on audio tape.)

McCraw, Vincent. Anxious Dixon on mission to cure D.C.'s ills. 1990. (April 17). *The Washington Times*.

Morris. M.L. (1992 October). "To Bea of Not To Bea? That is the Question," *Drumbeat*, 11.

Mullen, Robert. (1982). *Black Communications*: Washington, D.C. University Press of America.

Nelson, William E. (1977). *Electing Black Mayors: Political Action in the Black Community*. Columbus. Ohio State University Press.

Nelson, William E. (2000*). Black Atlantic Politics: Dilemmas of Political Empowerment in Boston and Liverpool*. Albany, N.Y.: State University of New York Press.

Randolph, Laura B. "Mayor Sharon Pratt Kelly on Her Marriage, Her Mission, and Her Midlife Transformation," *Ebony*, February 1992: 27-34.

Riffe, Daniel, et. al. (1990). Black elected officeholders find white press coverage insensitive, incomplete, and inappropriate. *Howard Journal of Communications*, 2, 4, Fall) 397-406.

Rustin, Bayard. (1965). From protest to politics: The future of the Civil Rights Movement. *Commentary*. February.

Shabazz, Hanifah. (1993). Personal interview. (recorded on audiotape by Deborah F. Atwater). 25 October.

Sheridan, Earl. (Nov. 1996). The new accommodationists. *Journal of Black Studies*. Vol.27, no.2: 152-171.

Sills, James H. (1993). Personal interview. (recorded on audiotape by Deborah F. Atwater). 21 October.

Sills, James H. (1993). *Wilmington: A New Spirit~A New Commitment: Inaugural Ceremony.* 5 January- Official Inaugural Souvenir Booklet.

Sylvie, George. (1995). Black mayoral candidates and the press: Running for coverage. *Howard Journal of Communications.* 6 (1&2) October 89-101.

The Town of Glenarden's 50ᵗʰ Anniversary Celebration Booklet, Town of Glenarden, 8600 Glenarden Parkway, Glenarden, MD 20706. (1989).

Thompson, Aaron. (1993). Personal interview. (recorded on audiotape by Deborah F. Atwater.) 20, October.

Thompson, Chris. (December 12, 2005). Rise of new Black leaders. *The Express Times.* Easton, PA.

Time, November 7, 1983, May 16, 1983.

Vaca, Nicolas C. (2004). *The Presumed Alliance: The Unspoken Conflict Between Latinos and Blacks and What it Means for America.* New York, New York, Harper Collins.

Washington, Linn. (1993). Personal Interview. (recorded on audio tape by Deborah F. Atwater). 29, September, Philadelphia, PA.

Weinberg, Kenneth G. (1968). *Black Victory: Carl Stokes and the Winning of Cleveland.* Chicago: Quadrangle Books.

White, Theodore. (1982). *America in Search of Itself: The Making of the President 1956-1980.* New York, New York: Harper & Row.

Wilson, Charles P. (1993). Wilmington under Sills. *Delaware Today,* January 28-32, 43- 48, 82.

Wilson, Marvin. (1994). Personal interview. (recorded on audiotape by Deborah F. Atwater). 3 June.

Index

Breinigsville, PA USA
17 August 2010
243717BV00003B/1/P